HAL LEONARD

FOLK BANJO METHOD

For 5-String Banjo

BY MICHAEL BREMER

ISBN 978-1-4803-6115-7

7777 W. BLUEMOUND RD. P.O. BOX 13819 MILWAUKEE, WI 53213

In Australia Contact:
Hal Leonard Australia Pty. Ltd.
4 Lentara Court
Cheltenham, Victoria, 3192 Australia
Email: ausadmin@halleonard.com.au

Visit Hal Leonard Online at
www.halleonard.com

CONTENTS

INTRODUCTION

WHAT IS FOLK STYLE BANJO?

There isn't a single folk style of banjo, and there's no "one way" to play folk music on the banjo. The folk banjo tradition includes many styles—strumming, Seeger-style picking, Southern clawhammer, Scruggs-style bluegrass picking, and everything in between. It's so rich and varied that it can't be covered in a dozen books, much less a single one.

So with this beginning book, you'll learn enough chords, strums, techniques, and picking patterns that you'll be able to play a few thousand songs. (Not a bad start.) Plus, you'll know the basics so you'll be ready to move on to any number of advanced techniques whenever you want.

FOR THAT MATTER, WHAT IS FOLK MUSIC?

Some say folk music is *traditional music*—i.e., old songs and tunes, many with unknown authors, that have stood the test of time. To some, folk music is the singers and singer-songwriters of the '50s and '60s, including greats like Bob Dylan, Judy Collins, Joan Baez, Gordon Lightfoot, Peter, Paul, and Mary, Pete Seeger, and many more.

To others, folk music is just "music that folks play." For a long time, folk music was an activity shared by families, friends, and communities. It wasn't a commercial product; it was just what people did to entertain themselves. It wasn't performance as much as it was group participation. Everyone played, sang, danced, or clapped.

THE SONGS IN THIS BOOK

In this book, we'll use traditional songs as the learning examples, but all the chords, rhythms, and techniques will be applicable to songs of the past, present, and future.

I chose older songs that many people will already be familiar with. Songs are easier to learn if you've heard them before and can already hum the tune. If they're new to you, then find a recording or a video and listen to them a few times before you learn to play them.

About the Audio

The accompanying audio demonstrates short versions of each of the songs, as well as all the exercises and progressions in this book. Note that, even though some of the exercises may show repeat signs, the audio tracks will normally ignore these.

It may be helpful to listen to these examples before you try to play them. In songs where the banjo plays the melody, there will be no vocals, so you can hear the banjo clearly. When the banjo just plays chords—either strumming or picking—there will be vocals mixed very low, again, so you can hear the banjo clearly.

To access the audio examples that accompany this book, simply go to **www.halleonard.com/mylibrary** and enter the code found on page 1. The examples that include audio are marked with an icon throughout the book.

WHAT YOU'LL NEED

Here's everything you'll need, and a few extras that are helpful.

- A five-string banjo

- An electronic tuner—preferably a clip-on tuner

- At least one ear (two are even better)

Useful options:

- Strap

- Capo

- 5th-string hooks

- Metronome

What About Picks?

Picks are a matter of preference. Some people use them, and some don't. They're necessary for some folk styles and impossible for others. Here's a quick run-down:

Flatpicks are not traditionally used with the five-string banjo, but they're used by four-string players to great effect for strumming. If you're a guitar player and you like playing with a pick, then go ahead and use one for the basic strumming parts of the book. You may get better results with a thin pick, because banjo strings are lighter and looser than guitar strings. One warning: many folk banjo styles, including some in this book, just don't work with a flatpick, so spend at least some time strumming without them.

Thumbpicks are used by some players in various styles to bring out melody notes between strums or along with fingerpicking.

Thumbpicks and fingerpicks are used by many players and are required for Scruggs-style bluegrass picking. The metal fingerpicks beloved by bluegrass players give your picking a clean, bright, loud sound, but they'll catch on the strings if you try to strum with them. There are some newer fingerpicks that allow picking and strumming. You can check them out online or in your favorite music store.

There are some parts of this book that will work with fingerpicks and others that won't.

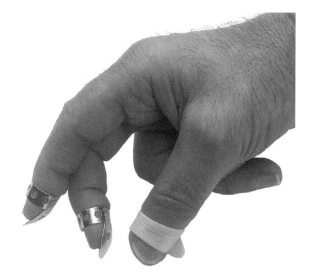

Bluegrass players and many folk players use a plastic thumbpick and two metal fingerpicks.

HOW TO PRACTICE

Learning to play involves both mental and physical aspects. Mentally, you'll learn chord shapes, progressions, and strumming and picking patterns. Physically, you have to build the coordination to play the music. Both of these aspects require some practice. When you schedule your practice time, it's important to know that you'll learn more and learn faster if you practice a few minutes every day than if you practice for hours only once a week.

BANJO PARTS AND TERMINOLOGY

Here are some basic terms and definitions that will help you understand the banjo.

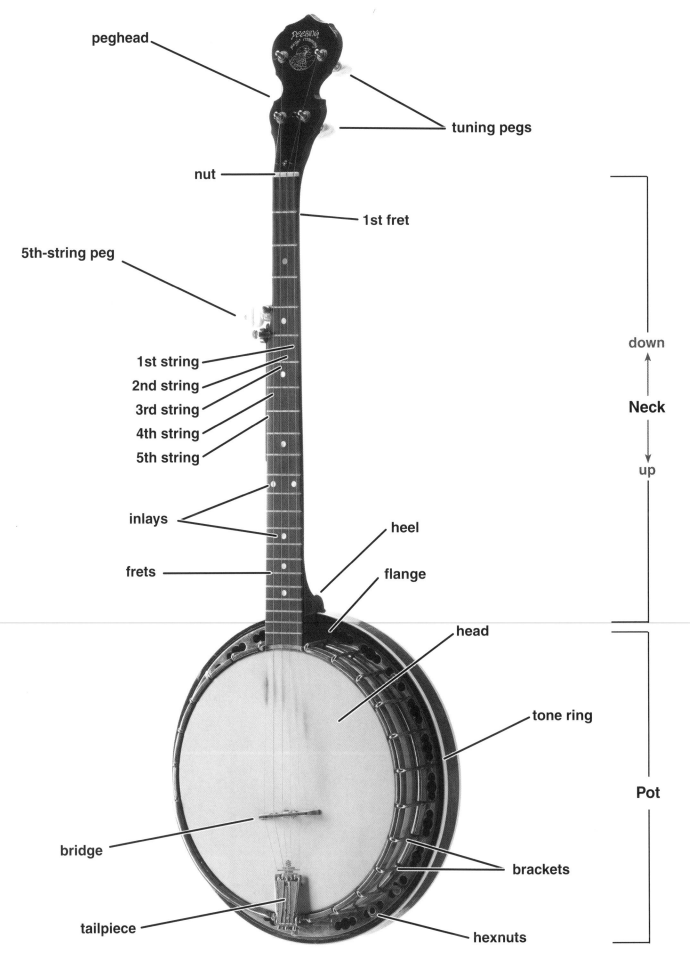

peghead

tuning pegs

nut

1st fret

5th-string peg

down

Neck

1st string

2nd string

3rd string

4th string

5th string

up

inlays

heel

frets

flange

head

tone ring

Pot

bridge

brackets

tailpiece

hexnuts

The banjo has two main sections: the *neck* and the *pot*. Both sections are made of many parts. When talking about the neck, up and down refer to the *pitch*, not the physical direction, so it may be confusing at first.

The *peg head* holds four of the five *tuning pegs*. The *5th-string tuning peg* is on the side of the neck.

Strings are numbered, from 1 to 5 in the order shown. Strings are held onto the banjo by the tuning pegs and the *tailpiece*. They are stretched over the *nut* and the *bridge*, which sits on the *head* (like a drum head).

Different banjos have different numbers of *frets* (some have no frets). The 1st fret is the one closest to the *nut*.

Most banjos have some sort of inlay marking to help you locate different frets. They are almost always on the 5th, 7th, and 12th frets, but may also be at the 3rd, 9th, 10th, or other frets.

Banjos often have *hooks* or other devices to quickly shorten and re-tune the 5th string. The hand you use to hold the strings onto the neck is the *fretting hand*. Right-handed people fret with their left hands; left-handed people fret with their right hands. The fret-hand fingers are numbered: index = 1, middle = 2, ring = 3, and pinky = 4.

The hand you use to hit, strum, or pluck the strings is the *striking hand*. Right-handed people strike with their right hands; left-handed people strike with their left hands. The striking-hand fingers are assigned letters: thumb = t, index = i, and middle = m.

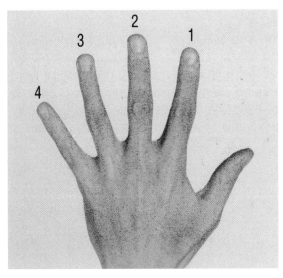

Fretting Hand

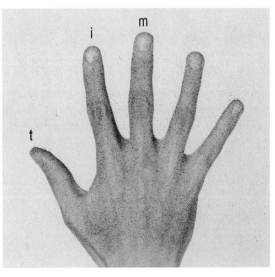

Striking Hand

CHAPTER 1: TUNING THE BANJO

In spite of—or maybe even because of—all the banjo jokes going around, it's important for us to play in tune. Today, because electronic tuners are so inexpensive, tuning is easier than ever.

Five-string banjos can be, and often are, tuned in many different ways. By this I mean the strings can be set to different notes, depending on what key you want to play in or what mood you want to set. It's not unusual to change the note of a string now and then just to make a song easier to play. These days, the most common way to tune a five-string banjo, and the tuning you'll be using in this book, is called *open G*. The strings are tuned so that when you play all the strings with no fingers fretting them (open), it plays a G chord.

The notes of these strings are g D G B D. The lowercase g is the shorter 5th string.

Here's a diagram that shows how it looks on a banjo:

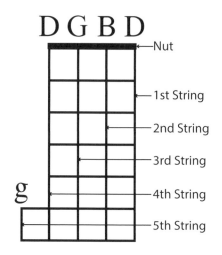

By far the quickest and easiest way to tune, especially for beginners, is to use an electronic tuner. Since they're easy to find, very inexpensive, and reasonably accurate, they're worth the investment. There are many types of tuners and they're all a little different, but all have enough in common with each other that if you can use one, you can use any of them. Which one should you buy? I recommend one of the many that clip onto the banjo head and pick up the sound directly as opposed to the ones that use a microphone and do not attach to the banjo. The advantage is that these only pick up the sound from your instrument, so it's easier to tune in a noisy environment, like a jam or class where there are lots of instruments tuning up.

Korg AW2 Clip-On Chromatic Tuner

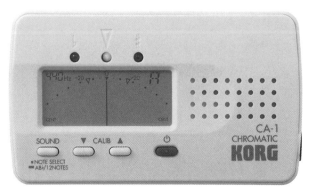

Korg CA-1 Chromatic Tuner

In general, to use a clip-on tuner:

1. Clip it onto your peg head so you can see the readout.

2. Turn it on.

3. Strike or pluck one string.

   - The tuner will display the note that that string is closest to, and some sort of meter to show if the pitch is *sharp* (too high) or *flat* (too low).

In Tune   Flat

4. Turn the tuning peg for that string until the string is in tune.

5. Repeat for all the other strings.

6. Turn the tuner off to save the battery.

Hints:

- The string will stay in tune better if you tune it up to the proper pitch rather than down to it. So if the string is sharp (too high), first lower it below the proper pitch then raise it.

- Make sure the note that the tuner displays is the right one—if the string is far out of tune, it could be closer to a different note.

- Take your time and don't get frustrated. Tuning, even with an electronic tuner, is a skill that takes a little time to master.

You can also tune by ear, matching the pitch to notes from a pitch pipe, piano, or guitar. Or you can use a pitch pipe or any other instrument to get one string in tune, and then tune the other strings relative to that one. Tuning by matching notes is a good way to develop your ear, but using a tuner is much quicker and easier.

CHAPTER 2:
BASIC CHORDS IN THE KEY OF G

For now, we'll learn to play in the key of G. This is because many good songs and tunes are often played in G (not to mention your banjo is tuned to open G, so playing in the key of G is the easiest).

THE POWER OF THREE (CHORDS)

Thousands of songs can be played using only three (sometimes only two) chords. Later on, you'll learn more chords, but for now you only have to learn three.

The three most important chords in the key of G are G, C, and D. Often D7, a variant of D, is used instead. It has a good sound and is very easy to finger on banjo in this tuning, so we'll use it here.

 FIRST CHORDS

Here are diagrams showing how to play your first three chords:

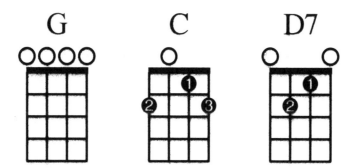

From right to left, strings 1–4 are represented here (5th string is not shown). The thick line at the top is the nut, so these chords are played at the end of the neck in "open position." The circles above the nuts tell you to play those strings open (no fingers on frets). The numbers inside the circles on the strings tell you what finger of your fretting hand to use: 1=index, 2=middle, 3=ring. Notice that the G chord doesn't require any fingers at all—so you already know it!

To play a chord, fret the notes with your fretting hand (your left hand if you're right-handed) and strike the strings with your other hand. To strike the strings, brush across all five of them in a smooth, downward motion with the back of one or more fingernails. (Typically, the open 5th string is strummed as well.) When you fret, put your finger close to the fret and press hard enough to get a clean, clear sound—but not so hard that you pull the string out of tune or hurt your fingers!

Take a little time now and work on playing each of these three chords one at a time. All the notes should sound clear, with no buzzing. If it's not clear, try moving your fingers closer to the fret and maybe press a little harder on the strings. Play the strings one at a time until you locate the problem note and then adjust your fingers as necessary to produce a clean note. The chords should sound like the example on the audio.

Once you can play each chord cleanly, tackle the following exercises to teach your fingers to change chords. For each of these exercises, strum each chord four times and then change to the next chord. Each slash mark or chord letter indicates *one* strum. Start very slowly. When you can change chords smoothly, speed it up a little. The more time and effort you put into these exercises, the easier it'll be to learn songs.

🔊 CHORD EXERCISE 1

||: G / / / | C / / / | G / / / | C / / / :||

COUNT: 1 2 3 4 1 2 3 4 1 2 3 4 1 2 3 4

🔊 CHORD EXERCISE 2

||: G / / / | D7 / / / | G / / / | D7 / / / :||

1 2 3 4 1 2 3 4 1 2 3 4 1 2 3 4

🔊 CHORD EXERCISE 3

||: C / / / | D7 / / / | C / / / | D7 / / / :||

1 2 3 4 1 2 3 4 1 2 3 4 1 2 3 4

🔊 CHORD EXERCISE 4

||: G / / / | C / / / | D7 / / / | G / / / :||

1 2 3 4 1 2 3 4 1 2 3 4 1 2 3 4

🔊 CHORD EXERCISE 5

||: G / / / | D7 / / / | C / / / | G / / / :||

1 2 3 4 1 2 3 4 1 2 3 4 1 2 3 4

🔊 CHORD EXERCISE 6

||: C / / / | G / / / | D7 / / / | G / / / :||

1 2 3 4 1 2 3 4 1 2 3 4 1 2 3 4

CHAPTER 3: STRUMMING PATTERNS AND VARIATIONS

Now that you can play a few chords and change between them smoothly, it's time to add some more interest to your playing with strumming patterns and variations.

WHERE TO STRUM

You can get a wide range of tones from your banjo by strumming in different places. The closer you strum to the bridge, the brighter and sharper the tone will be. The farther you strum from the bridge, the mellower the tone. So, for a high-energy song, you may want to strum close to the bridge. For a slow, sweet song, however, try strumming near the neck.

This applies to playing styles other than strumming as well; most bluegrass players generally want that bright tone, so they pick near the bridge. Many clawhammer players want a mellower tone, though, so they strike the strings over the fingerboard near where it meets the pot.

STRUMMING PATTERNS

The most important thing about strumming is to keep a steady rhythm. Just playing four simple down-strums, as you have in the previous exercises—at a steady tempo with smooth chord changes—sounds better than all sorts of fancy up- and down-strumming if the timing isn't steady.

So far, for each count of four, you've played four down-strums, all on the beat. This can be notated in *tablature* (or *tab*) as shown below. The lines represent strings 1 to 5, from top to bottom. The numbers on the strings tell you what fret to put your finger on. Since this is a G chord, you don't need any fretting fingers, and you play all five strings open. The ⊓ symbol means to strum downward (toward the floor).

🔊 STRUM 1

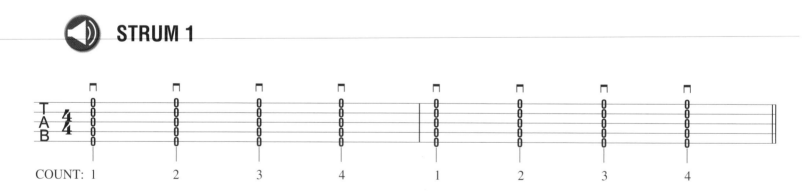

Listen to the audio example and try it, counting out loud as you do. If you don't hit all the strings every strum, that's OK. With strumming, a steady rhythm is more important than hitting all the strings.

EXPANDING THE COUNT

Next, we'll expand the count. You'll play the exact same strum but add the word "and" between each number of the count.

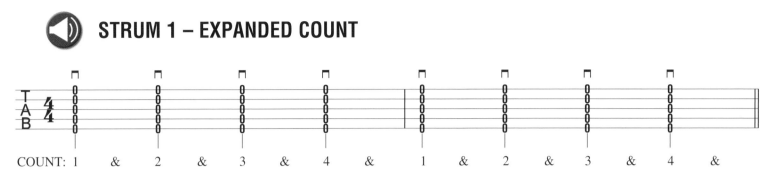

STRUM 1 – EXPANDED COUNT

Listen to the audio and then play—and say—this for a while. The "ands" are important: they represent where you'll add the up-strums.

UP-STRUMS

An up-strum is just what it sounds like: you strum upward instead of downward. When you up-strum, you don't have to strum all the strings: just strings 1, 2, and 3, or even just strings 1 and 2. Steady rhythm is more important than hitting the same exact strings. In the notation below, the V symbol indicates an up-strum.

Here are a number of different ways to add up-strums:

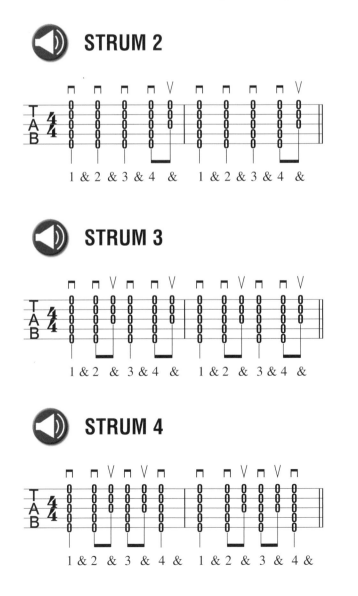

STRUM 2

STRUM 3

STRUM 4

STRUM 5

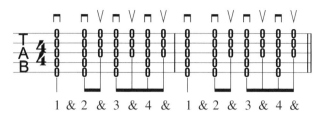

A good way to add interest to strumming is to skip some down-strums, as in these patterns:

STRUM 6

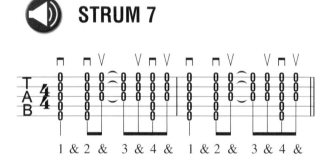

STRUM 7

BREAKING UP THE DOWN-STRUM

Another way to give your strum patterns more interest is to break up the down-strum and either strum strings 5, 4, and 3 or strings 3, 2, and 1. Notice that they're all down-strums—and don't worry about hitting the same exact strings every time.

STRUM 8

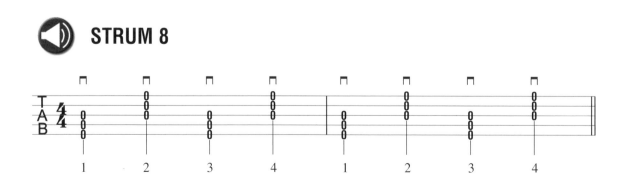

Here are a couple of variations that add some up-strums. You don't have to be precisely accurate on hitting the exact strings, but try to be close. Pay attention to the strum direction (up or down).

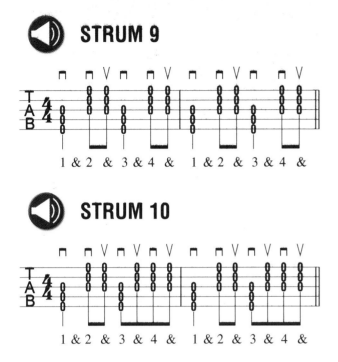

STRUM 9

STRUM 10

WALTZING: THE THREE COUNT

Many great songs and tunes are *waltzes*, meaning you count them "1, 2, 3, 1, 2, 3" instead of "1, 2, 3, 4, 1, 2, 3, 4." Here are a couple of strumming patterns that work well for waltzes. As before, count the beats as you play to help you lock in the rhythm.

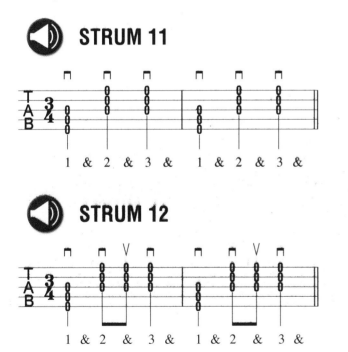

STRUM 11

STRUM 12

PUTTING YOUR STRUMS TO WORK

Now that you're at least familiar with most of these strums, put them to work. Choose your favorite strums—including the waltz strums—and apply them to all of the chord changing exercises in Chapter 2.

Of course, these examples represent only a few of the possible strumming patterns you can play. Take some time to experiment and come up with a few patterns of your own.

CHAPTER 4: YOUR FIRST SONGS

By now, you know some chords and strum patterns, and you're ready to learn a few songs. If you've spent time on the previous chapters, these songs won't be a problem for you (but they will take a little time and effort). If you're not familiar with a song, listen to it a few times before you try to play it.

For each song, you'll be given one or more recommended strumming patterns, but feel free to try other patterns, including your own. The goal here is to keep a steady rhythm and have some fun. Chords are only given when they change, so keep playing the same chord until you see a new one. Try playing the chords all the way through a few times while counting out loud and then try singing while you play.

A simple version of the melody will be shown in tablature, showing the string and fret for each given melody note. You don't need to play the notes on the banjo (yet), but they're there in case you need help finding the notes to sing.

The first two songs are:

- "Down in the Valley" – This is a traditional American folk song also known as "Birmingham Jail." A good song to start with, it has only two chords. Each measure of this song has three counts.

- "Will the Circle Be Unbroken" – This is a standard song in the bluegrass world as well as old time and general folk circles. It began as a Christian hymn by Ada R. Habershon and Charles H. Gabriel in 1907 and evolved over the years to become one of the most popular gospel songs around.

By the time you can play these two songs steadily and comfortably with strumming patterns, you'll be ready to move on to the next step and start fancying up your playing. But don't forget the simple strum; sometimes it's the best way to play. It has a lot of energy and can really drive a song, supporting one singer or a dozen. It's also a useful technique to strum simply while singing and then play in a more melodic way for an instrumental break (more on that later).

If you want to get more strumming practice in, apply strum patterns to any of the other songs in this book or any other songs you want to play.

Recommended strum pattern:

DOWN IN THE VALLEY STRUM

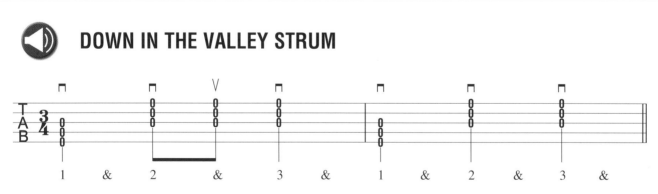

DOWN IN THE VALLEY

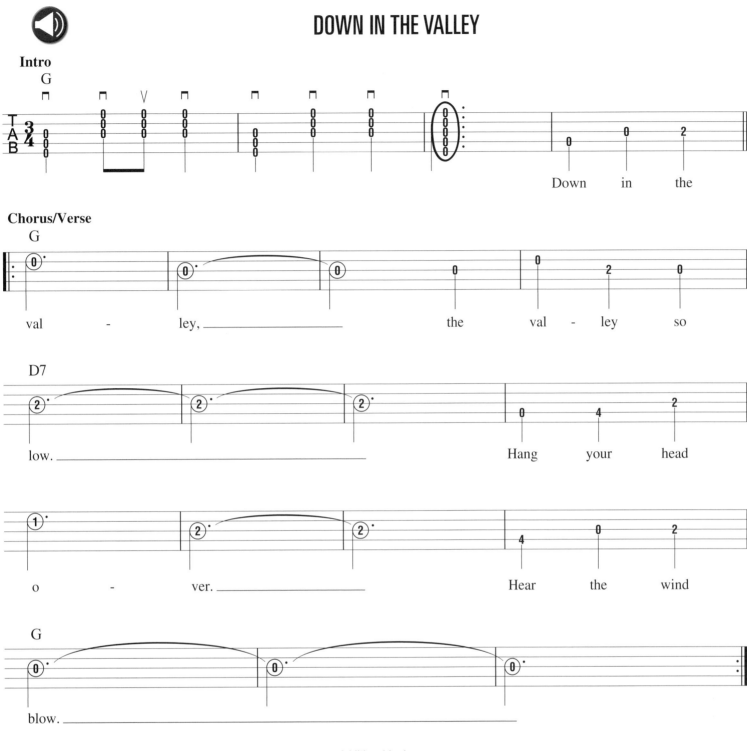

Additional Lyrics:

Roses love sunshine; violets love dew.
Angels in heaven know I love you.
Know I love you, dear, know I love you,
Angels in heaven know I love you.

Write me a letter; send it by mail.
Send it in care of the Birmingham jail.
Birmingham jail, dear, Birmingham jail,
Send it in care of the Birmingham jail.

Playing Notes:

- The introduction (intro) establishes the tempo and the strumming pattern. The banjo then stops, letting the voice begin the song alone. Listen to the audio to hear how to play it.

- Repeat the verse/chorus section while you sing the additional verses.

Recommended strum patterns (switch between them as you like):

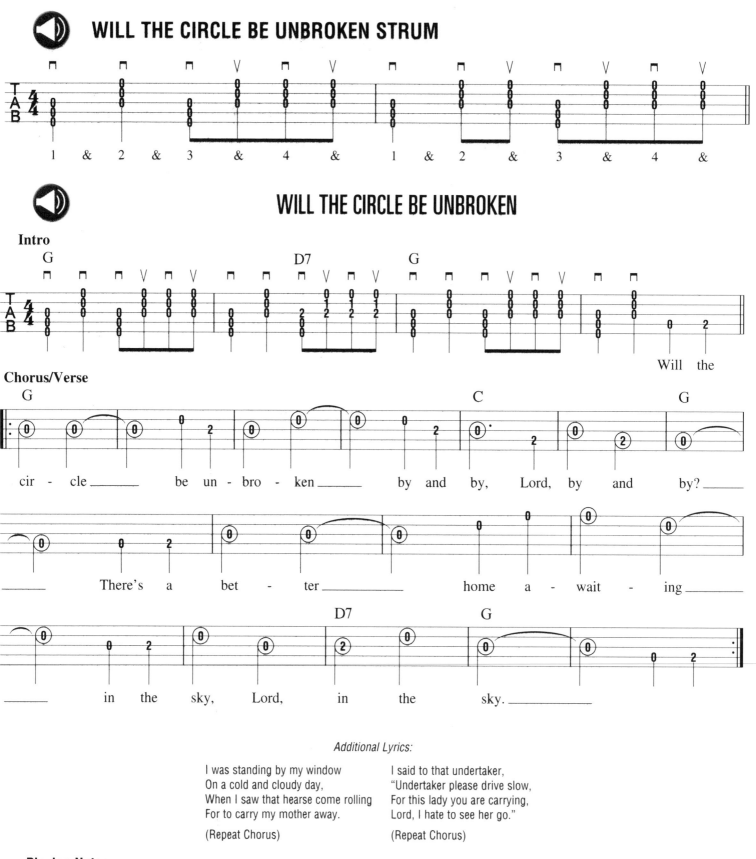

WILL THE CIRCLE BE UNBROKEN STRUM

WILL THE CIRCLE BE UNBROKEN

Intro

Chorus/Verse

cir - cle ____ be un - bro - ken ____ by and by, Lord, by and by?

____ There's a bet - ter ____ home a - wait - ing ____

____ in the sky, Lord, in the sky. ____

Additional Lyrics:

I was standing by my window
On a cold and cloudy day,
When I saw that hearse come rolling
For to carry my mother away.

(Repeat Chorus)

I said to that undertaker,
"Undertaker please drive slow,
For this lady you are carrying,
Lord, I hate to see her go."

(Repeat Chorus)

Playing Notes:

- The song starts with a chorus, and you sing a chorus after every verse. The verse and chorus have the same chords and melody, but you can change the strum pattern if you want to emphasize the difference.

- A strum for the intro is given. You can stop strumming for the first two words or keep the strumming going—your choice.

CHAPTER 5: STRUM-THUMB

The 5th string defines the sound of the five-string banjo. So far, we've just strummed it along with other strings. That's OK, but sometimes you may want to really let that 5th string ring. One way to do this is to use the strumming patterns like the ones you've already used, but replace the up-strums with a thumb-pluck on the 5th string. Here are three patterns to practice until you get a good feel for the strum-thumb. It wouldn't hurt to count along with these.

One thing to watch for: previously on the lower-string strums, you hit strings 5, 4, and 3. Here, try instead to hit strings 4, 3, and 2. This way, when you hit the 5th string, it really stands out. But don't fret too much about hitting the 5th string on the strum; it'll still sound good.

STRUM-THUMB 1

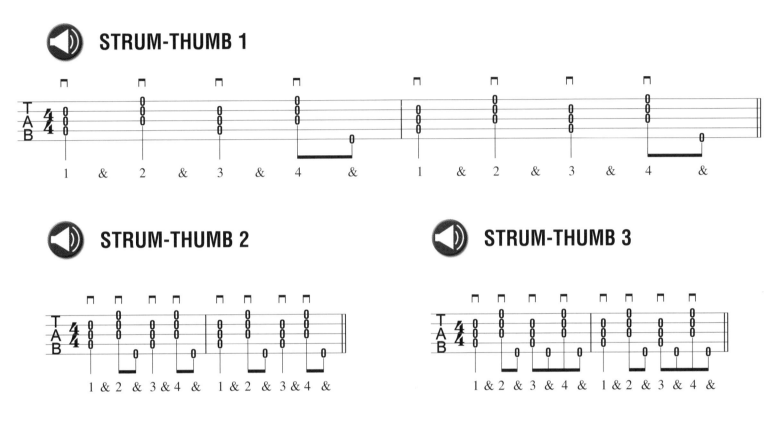

STRUM-THUMB 2

STRUM-THUMB 3

Here's a strum-thumb pattern with a three count that would work for songs like "Down in the Valley."

STRUM-THUMB 4

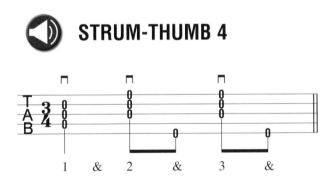

The strum-thumb is easiest to do if you plant your thumb on the 5th string as you make the previous strum. So, in Strum-Thumb 1 above, for beats 1, 2, and 3, you'd strum down as you have before. But on beat 4, as you strum down, catch your thumb on the 5th string. On the "and," just lightly pluck the 5th string as you raise your hand for the next down-strum. This is a little tricky, but it sounds good once you get it, so take your time and be patient.

Try playing both songs from Chapter 3 and the chord exercises from Chapter 2 using these strum-thumb patterns.

CHAPTER 6: NOTE-STRUM AND NOTE-STRUM-THUMB

The next step in the growth of your playing is to gain a little more control of your striking hand and mix single notes with multi-string strums. To do this, look back at the strumming patterns you've already learned and change them up a bit: replace the short down-strum on beats 1 and 3 with a single note on the 4th string. For instance, this pattern:

STRUM 8 – REVISITED

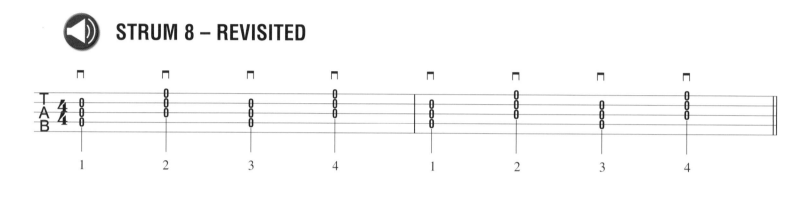

Becomes this:

NOTE-STRUM 1

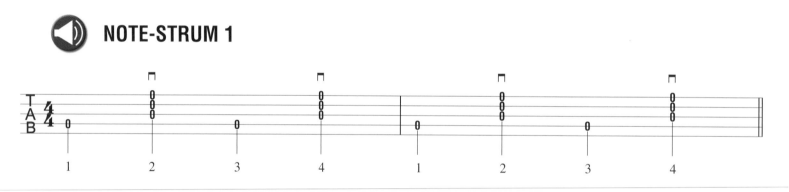

Notice that there's no direction indicator for the notes on beats 1 and 3. That's because you have a choice. You can:

- Hit the note in a downward motion as you would a strum, using the back of your fingernail (or flatpick)

- Hit the note in a downward direction using your thumb—with or without a thumbpick

- Pluck the string in an upward motion using your index finger

On a simple pattern like this, all of these techniques work well and they all sound nearly identical. They all have their uses and can all be developed into wonderfully musical techniques. But they don't all work all the time for all the things you may want to play—or that you'll find in this book. You owe it to yourself to at least try each of these techniques for a while and see which one, or better yet, which two or three, you prefer.

In that spirit, here are a few note-strum patterns for you to try—first as written here, and then apply them to the chord exercises in Chapter 2.

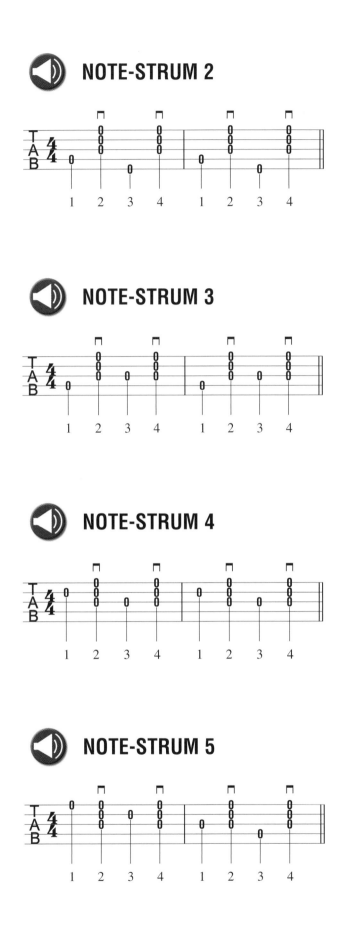

Here's a version of "Will the Circle Be Unbroken" using note-strum patterns. The words are shown where they are to be sung rhythmically, but the melody notes aren't shown. This may be easiest to play if you use your index finger (either striking down or plucking up) for most of the single notes and the thumb for the single notes on the 5th string, but try it any way you want.

WILL THE CIRCLE BE UNBROKEN — NOTE-STRUM

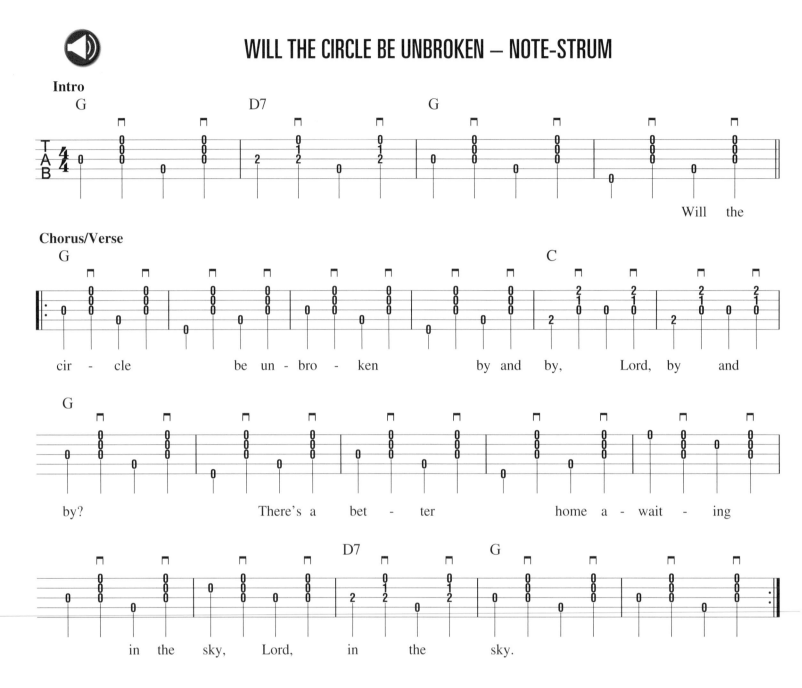

Now let's add some more 5th string to the mix using some note-strum-thumb patterns. These are best played without a flatpick or fingerpicks, but a thumbpick will work if that's your preference. The notes on beats 1 and 3 are best played with the index finger, either struck downward or plucked upward. The 5th string is played with the thumb. Again, the thumb notes are easier to play if you plant your thumb on the 5th string as you strum the strum just before the thumb.

NOTE-STRUM-THUMB 1

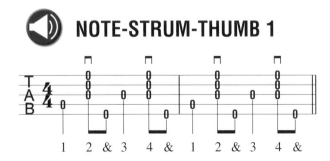

NOTE-STRUM-THUMB 2

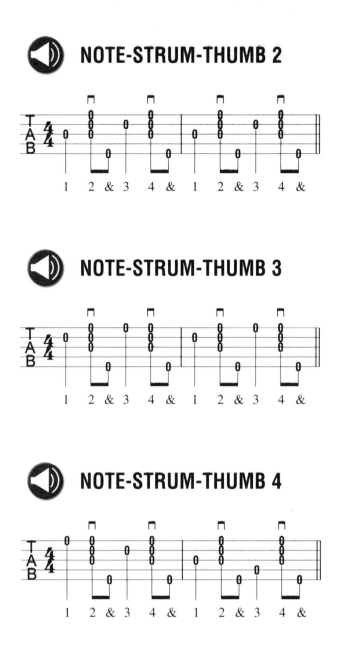

NOTE-STRUM-THUMB 3

NOTE-STRUM-THUMB 4

Here's some note-strum-thumb practice for songs with a three count.

NOTE-STRUM-THUMB 5

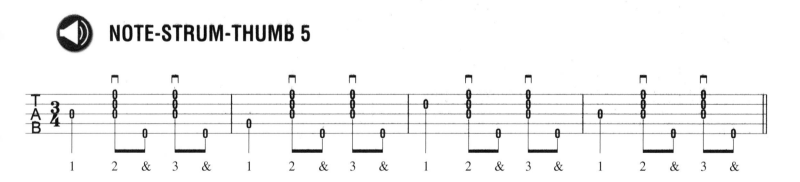

The more you practice these, the easier they get, so once you can play them smoothly, try them out on the chord exercises before you move on.

CHAPTER 7: ADDING MELODY TO NOTE-STRUM-THUMB

So far, we've maintained the strum on beats 2 and 4 throughout. Now, we'll loosen that up and play more melody notes, adding strums or strum-thumbs to fill in between the notes.

Let's revisit "Down in the Valley" and include the entire melody along with strum-thumbs filling in. All the strums are down-strums.

DOWN IN THE VALLEY — MELODY WITH STRUM-THUMB

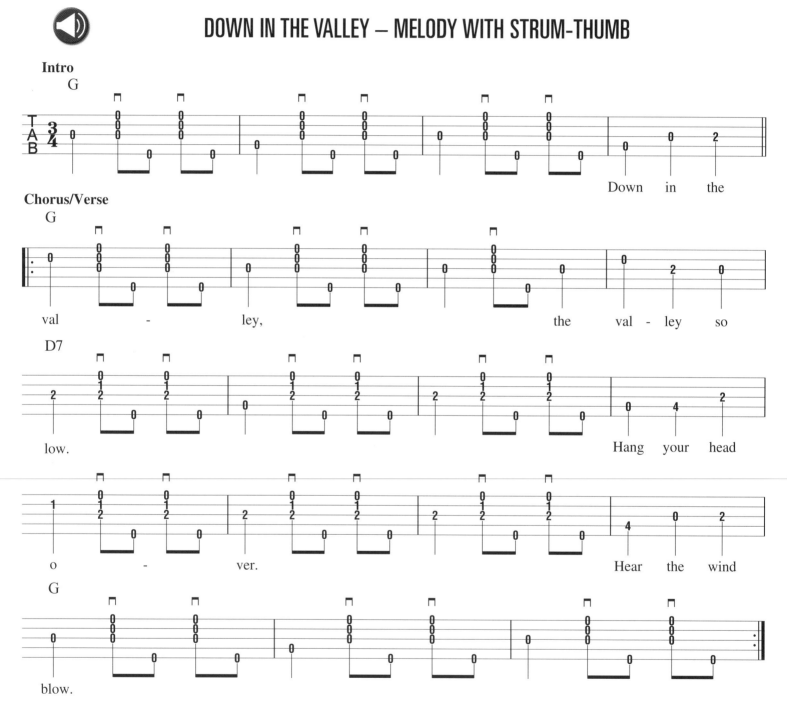

Playing Note:

- There are two places where you have to play the 4th fret of the 4th string. Try stretching your pinky to fret that note. If it's too uncomfortable, use your ring finger.

And here's "Will the Circle Be Unbroken" with the complete melody. All the strums are down-strums, so they aren't marked on the tab.

WILL THE CIRCLE BE UNBROKEN — MELODY WITH STRUM-THUMB

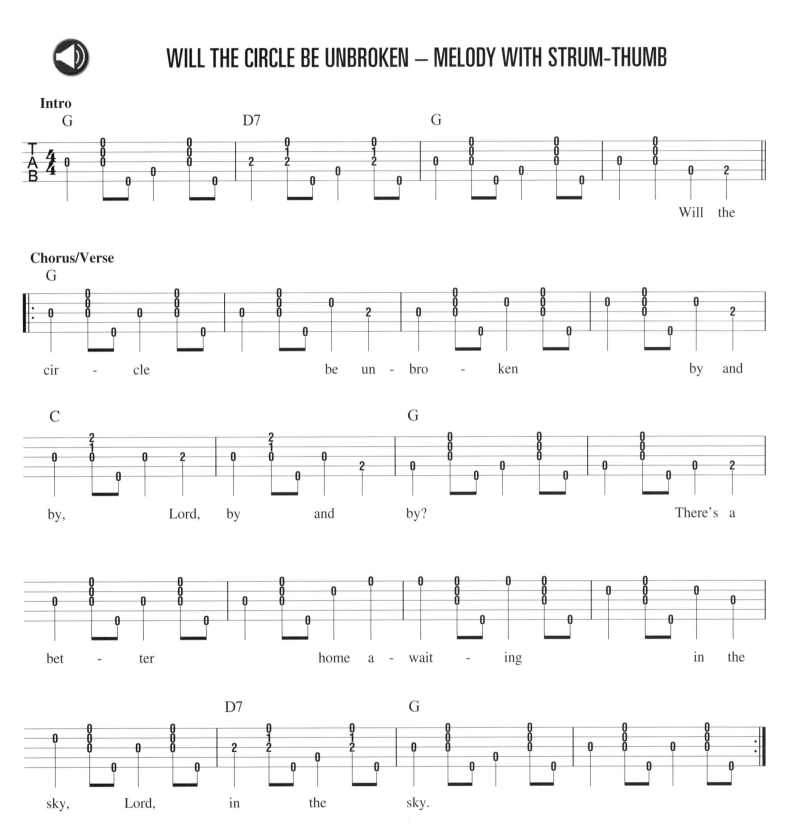

This technique of playing the melody notes and filling in with strums or strum-thumbs is a great way to play songs. You can play like this the whole time to guide singers with the melody, or you can strum simply while singing and then add the melody for an instrumental break.

CHAPTER 8:
HAMMER-ONS, PULL-OFFS, AND SLIDES

Hammer-ons, *pull-offs*, and *slides* are all signature sounds of the banjo. Listen to (or watch closely) any banjo player you like; they'll no doubt be using these three techniques.

HAMMER-ONS

A *hammer-on* is when you strike a note—open string or fretted one—and then "hammer" a fretting finger down on the same string at a higher fret. The result is two notes sounding (in succession) with one strike. Hammer-on close to the fret and use just enough force to get a clean sound.

Here's a quick exercise to help you get the feel of hammering-on. The curved line (called a *slur*) connecting the notes with the "h" above indicates a hammer-on. The small numbers above the notes indicate which fretting finger you should use (1 = index, 2 = middle, 3 = ring, 4 = pinky). Pay attention to the fingering. The last measure uses your pinky, which is awkward at first, but worth the effort. Strike or pluck the strings any way you want. Play this exercise slowly and cleanly.

▶ HAMMER-ON EXERCISE 1

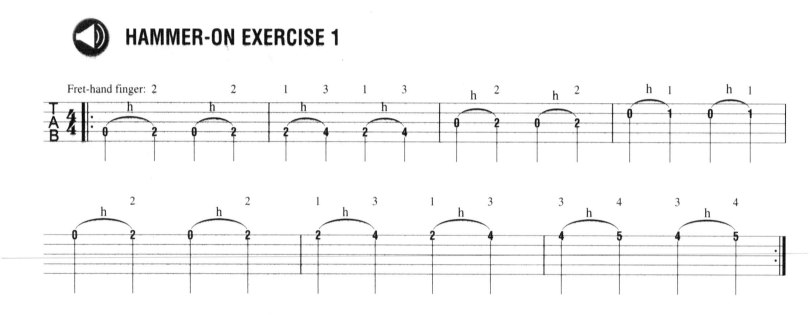

Now here's some hammering-on along with strum-thumbs. The hammers are all performed by finger 2 (the middle finger).

▶ HAMMER-ON EXERCISE 2

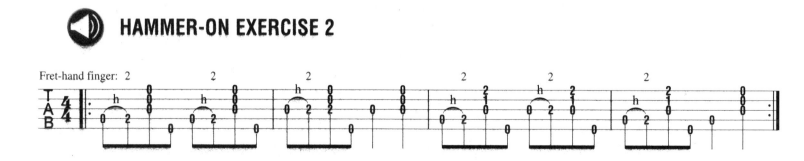

PULL-OFFS

A *pull-off* is kind of the opposite of a hammer-on. You play a fretted note and then use the fretting finger to play a note below it as you pull it off of the string. You can pull off to an open or fretted string. Again, the result is two notes from one strike.

Here's an exercise to help you get the hang of pulling off. The curved line with the "p" above it indicates a pull-off. Pay attention to the fingering and work that pinky!

PULL-OFF EXERCISE 1

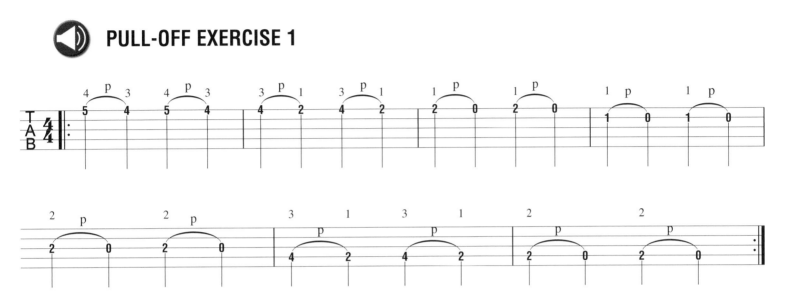

Now for some pulling-off along with strum-thumbs. The middle finger does most of the work here.

PULL-OFF EXERCISE 2

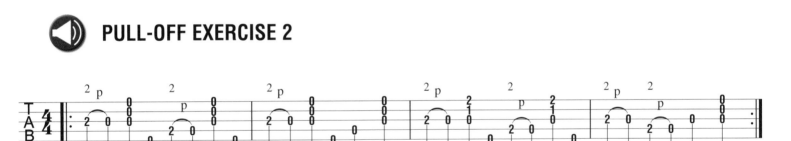

Next, here's a mix of hammering-on and pulling-off.

HAMMER & PULL EXERCISE

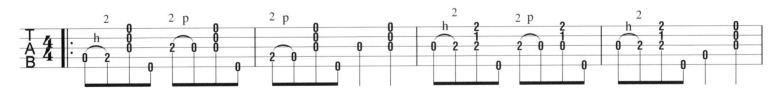

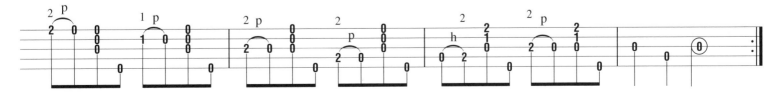

SLIDES

Another great-sounding technique you can use is the *slide*. To slide, play a fretted note and then slide the fretting finger up or down to another fret (or to an open string). Be sure to maintain pressure on the fretboard as you slide.

Here are two little exercises to help you get a feel for it. The diagonal line with an "sl" over it indicates a slide. Notice that sometimes you slide one fret and sometimes two or even more. You can perform all the slides here with the middle finger, but it wouldn't hurt to do this exercise using the index or ring finger as well.

SLIDE EXERCISE 1

SLIDE EXERCISE 2

"Cripple Creek" is a great traditional tune. It's sometimes sung but is very popular as an instrumental tune in both bluegrass and old-time jams. It has a form of AABB; you play the A part twice, the B part twice, and then repeat the whole thing.

Here's a way to play it using pull-offs and slides. Again, all the strums are down-strums.

CRIPPLE CREEK

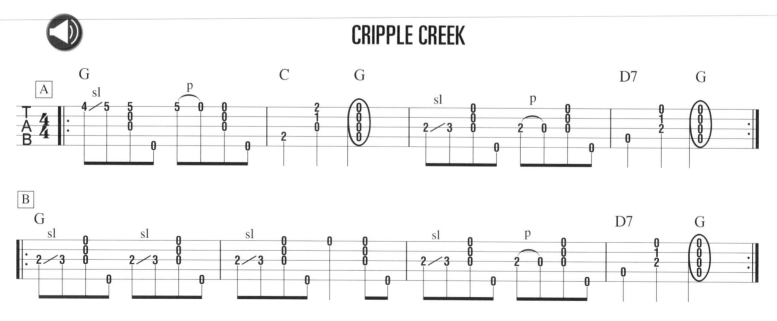

CHAPTER 9:
MORE SONGS IN THE KEY OF G

By now you can strum, strum-thumb, note-strum, and note-strum-thumb, and you can spice things up with hammer-ons, pull-offs, and slides. With these techniques and the three chords you know, you can play many hundreds of songs. But with just a few more chords, you can play many hundreds more.

In this chapter, you'll learn four more songs—some with the three chords you already know, and some with new chords. You can play each of the new songs in many different ways, depending on your preference and your skill level:

- Strum the chords using your favorite strum patterns (may be best while singing).

- Play the chords using note-strum, strum-thumb, or note-strum-thumb (while singing or as a solo).

- Play the melody notes and use strums and strum-thumbs to fill in between the notes.

For each song, you'll be given the chord names above the tab staff to use for strumming (and various note-strum and strum-thumb variations, as you see fit) while singing. Try a few patterns and see what works for you. For each song, there is also a tabbed-out arrangement with the words below. The arrangements will vary from simple to fancy, giving you a good sampling of different ways to play folk banjo.

If the down-up strums or strum-thumbs still give you trouble, then go ahead and play these songs with a simple, single down-strum in those spots for now. But go back and spend a little time with the exercises to build your down-up and strum-thumb skills. Before long, they'll find their way into your playing.

If you're a beginner, I recommend learning these, and other new songs, in stages.

1. First, listen to them until you can sing or at least hum them.

2. Play the chords simply—either with a strum, note-strum, or note-strum thumb—until you can play the song smoothly and comfortably.

3. Play the chords and sing or at least hum along.

4. Learn the arrangement provided here and use it either as an instrumental solo or a back up to your singing.

These arrangements are just one way to play the songs; once they're familiar to you and you can play them fairly smoothly, try your own variations. There's a reason they call it "playing" music—so play with it! Try out different things. Add hammer-ons, pull-offs, or slides. Change the strums. Use more or less thumb on the 5th string.

NEW CHORDS

Here are a few additional chords that are commonly used in songs in the key of G. We won't use all of them right now, but take the time to at least get familiar with them.

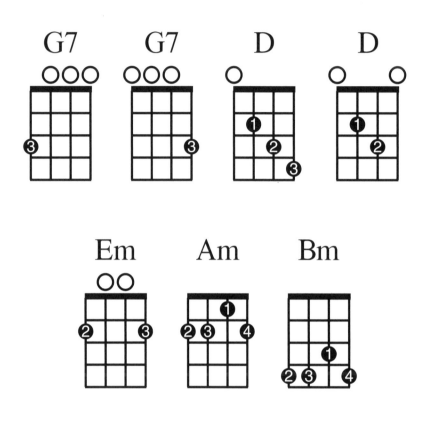

Playing Notes:

- Notice that there are two ways shown for both the G7 and the D. You can use either one, but depending on the song, one of the ways may sound better or help you play the melody note.

- The E minor chord (Em) is fingered just like the C chord but without the index finger.

- The A minor chord (Am) uses all four fingers of your fretting hand.

- The B minor chord (Bm) is fingered exactly like the Am, but all four fingers are placed two frets farther up the neck.

CHORD EXERCISES

Here are a few exercises to help you get used to playing these chords. Play them using any technique you want. The main thing to work on here is changing the chords smoothly enough to keep a steady rhythm.

Try Chord Exercise 7 with the first G7 and first D, and then with the second G7 and second D. Mix them up if you like.

CHORD EXERCISE 7

‖: G7 | D | G7 | D :‖

CHORD EXERCISE 8

‖: Em | Am | Em | Bm :‖

CHORD EXERCISE 9

‖: D | Am | D | Am :‖

CHORD EXERCISE 10

‖: D | Am | D | Bm :‖

"Oh! Susanna" is a song that many of us grew up with. Attributed to Stephen Foster and first published in 1848, it has a bouncy polka rhythm and some seriously silly lyrics—except, of course, for the line "with a banjo on my knee."

OH! SUSANNA

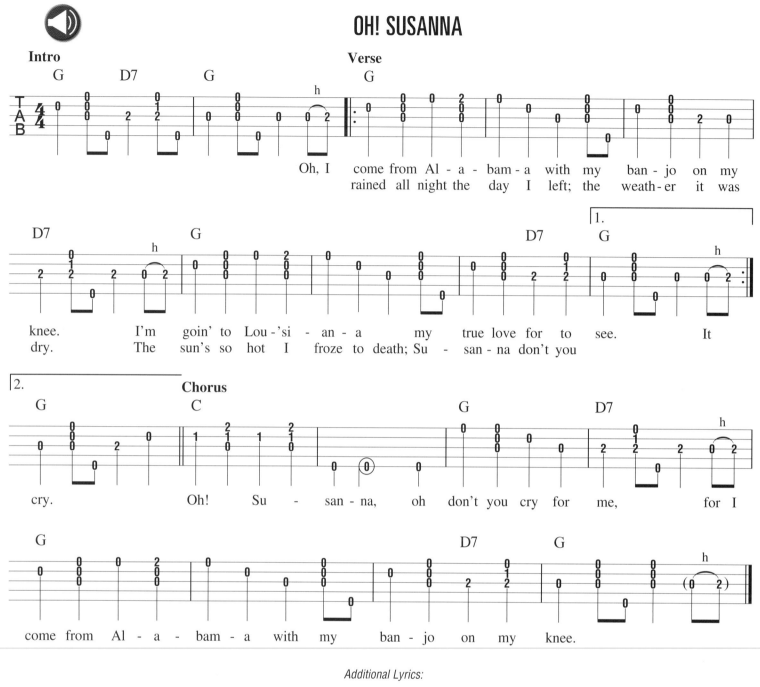

Additional Lyrics:

I had a dream the other night, when everything was still;
I thought I saw Susanna dear, a-coming down the hill.
A buckwheat cake was in her mouth; a tear was in her eye.
Says I, I'm coming from the south; Susanna, don't you cry.

(Repeat Chorus)

I soon will be in New Orleans, and then I'll look around.
And when I find Susanna, I'll fall upon the ground.
But if I do not find her, then I will surely die.
And when I'm dead and buried, oh, Susanna, don't you cry.

(Repeat Chorus)

Playing Notes:

- "Oh! Susanna" has the same three chords as the previous songs and is primarily played with notes and strums, with an occasional strum-thumb thrown in.

- All the strums are down-strums.

- You can play the individual notes either by striking down with the back of your nail or by plucking up.

- In the second measure of the chorus, where the words are "san-na, oh," play those three 5th-string notes with your thumb.

- In the last measure of the chorus, the last two notes lead back into the verse. To end the song, leave these two notes off.

"Red River Valley" is both a folk song and a cowboy song. Over the years, and in different locations, it has also been known as "Bright Sherman Valley," "Bright Little Valley," "Cowboy Love Song," and other names.

RED RIVER VALLEY

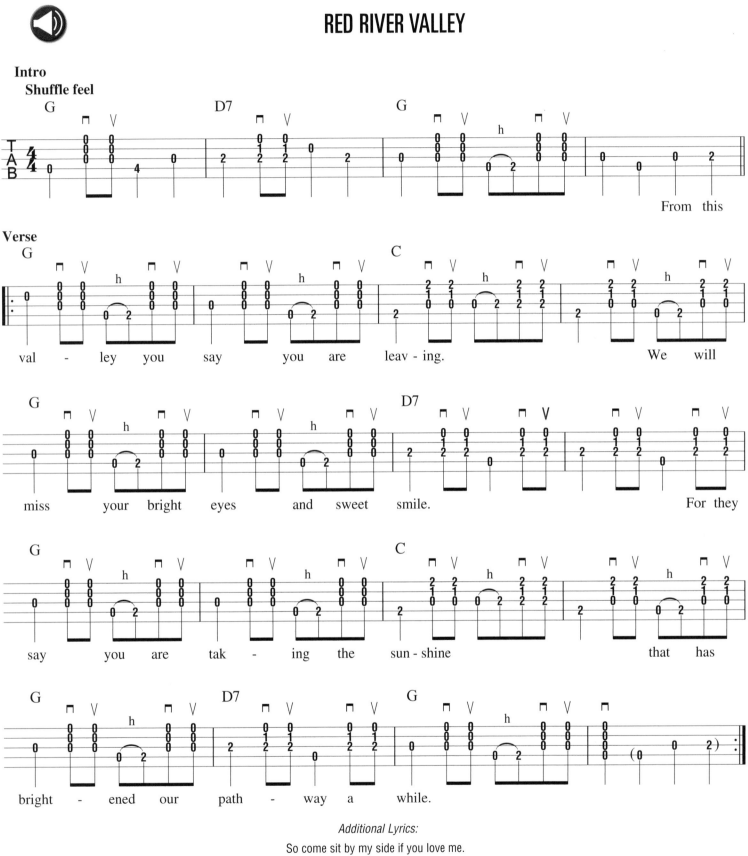

Additional Lyrics:

So come sit by my side if you love me.
Do not hasten to bid me adieu.
Just remember the Red River Valley
And the cowboy who loved you so true.

Playing Notes:

- The "Shuffle feel" indication at the beginning of "Red River Valley" tells you to play the down-up strums and hammer-ons in this song with a bouncy, lopsided feel. This is a very common sound, and one listen to the audio will make it perfectly clear.

- Other than the intro, this arrangement just outlines the melody and supports one or more singers with enough hammer-ons to add interest (and be fun to play).

- To give the song a "cowboy feel," this arrangement features notes and strums. But feel free to add strum-thumbs if you want.

- If the down-up strums give you trouble, you can skip the up-strums at first.

- The last three notes lead back to the beginning for the next verse. To end the song, leave these three notes off.

"Lonesome Road Blues," a traditional American song also known as "Goin' Down the Road Feeling Bad," among other names, has been recorded by everyone from Bill Monroe to Woody Guthrie to Elizabeth Cotten to the Grateful Dead.

LONESOME ROAD BLUES

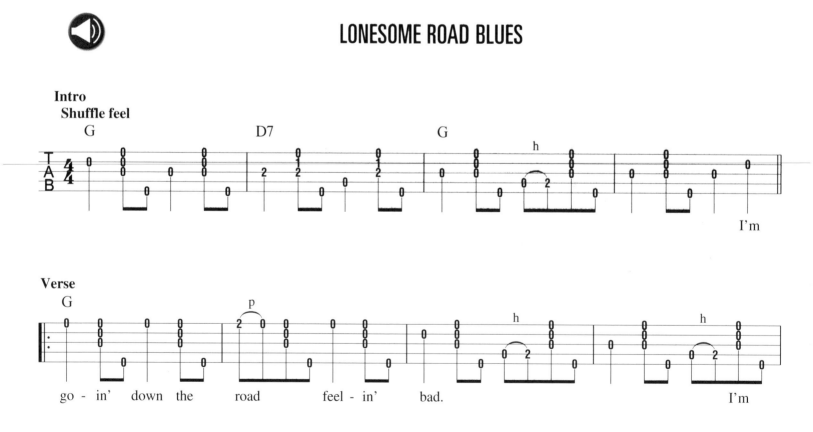

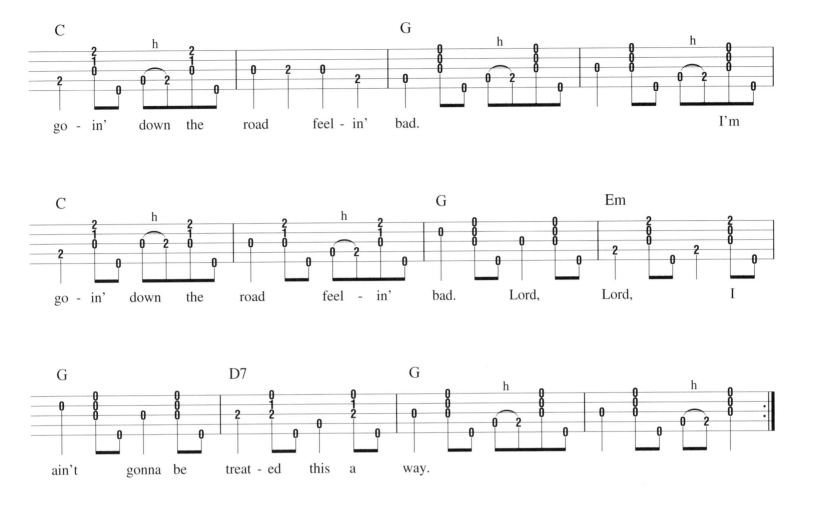

Additional Lyrics:

Got two dollar shoes on my feet.
Got two dollar shoes on my feet.
Two dollar shoes, they hurt my feet.
Lord, Lord, and I ain't gonna be treated this a way.

I'm going where the weather suits my clothes.
I'm going where the weather suits my clothes.
I'm going where the weather suits my clothes.
Lord, Lord, and I ain't gonna be treated this a way.

Playing Notes:

- This song includes the E minor chord (Em), just for a short while, but it adds a lot of flavor and interest.

- Again, for the single notes, you can strike down or pluck up.

"The Water Is Wide" has its roots in England and is known by other names, including "O Waly, Waly." It was first published in 1906 but still holds up today, both melodically and lyrically.

THE WATER IS WIDE

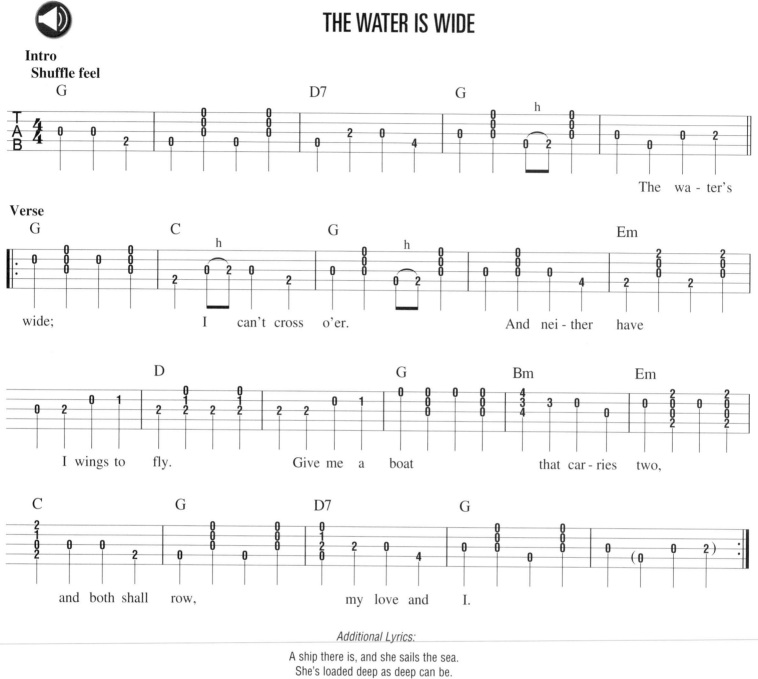

Additional Lyrics:

A ship there is, and she sails the sea.
She's loaded deep as deep can be.
But not so deep as the love I'm in.
I know not if I sink or swim.

Playing Notes:

- This is a slow, pretty song—one not usually considered a banjo song. But if you play it smoothly, it sounds great.

- Strike or pluck the strings far away from the bridge—even over the highest frets—to get a mellower tone.

- This song includes the Em chord and Bm chord.

- Watch for the places where a strum sounds on beat 1.

- Again, for the single notes, you can strike down or pluck up. Since there are no strum-thumbs, you can also play single notes with your thumb.

- The last three notes lead back to the beginning of the verse. To end the song, don't play these notes.

CHAPTER 10:
CHORDS AND SONGS IN THE KEY OF C

So far we've played everything in the key of G. But there are times when it's useful to play in other keys as well. Why play in other keys? For a number of reasons:

- If you want to play with other people (and that's at least half the fun of playing banjo), you have to be able to play in the keys they play in.

- Singers find it easier to sing in some keys and harder in others.

- Changing keys keeps things interesting for your audience, and it's fun.

Here's a chart that shows how to change the chords in the key of G to the key of C:

Numbers	I	ii	iii	IV	V	vi
Key of G	G	Am	Bm	C	D or D7	Em
Key of C	C	Dm	Em	F	G or G7	Am

The top row, labeled "Numbers," assigns a Roman numeral for each chord. The *root* (the key you are in) is the I (one) chord. The three most common chords are I, IV, and V in any key. These are shown in uppercase Roman numerals to indicate that they are major chords. The ii, iii, and vi chords are lowercase to indicate that they are minor chords.

To transpose from G to C, find the chord in the "Key of G" row and change it to the chord just below it in the "Key of C" row. For example, a song that has these chords in G:

$\|$: G $\qquad$ | Em $\qquad$ | C $\qquad$ | D7 $\qquad$:$\|$

Will have these chords in C:

$\|$: C $\qquad$ | Am $\qquad$ | F $\qquad$ | G7 $\qquad$:$\|$

NEW CHORDS FOR THE KEY OF C

The keys of G and C have many of the same chords. In fact, you already know most of them. The only new ones are D minor (Dm) and F. Here they are:

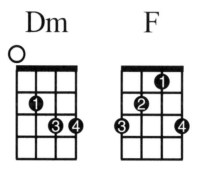

Note the fingering on the Dm. You can also finger it with fingers 1, 2, and 3, but this fingering leaves your middle finger available for melody notes on the 3rd and 4th strings. The F chord requires all four fingers.

The 5th string, which is tuned to a G, isn't in either Dm or F, but it doesn't sound bad; in fact, it adds a nice extra flavor to the chords. But you may want to try strumming these chords without the 5th string to get used to the basic Dm and F sounds.

CHORD EXERCISES

Here's an exercise to familiarize your fingers with the two new chords:

CHORD EXERCISE 11

‖: Dm | F | Dm | F :‖

Here are two more that are actually very common progressions for many songs from the '40s and '50s. They make great exercises for playing in the key of C.

CHORD EXERCISE 12

‖: C | Am | Dm | G :‖

CHORD EXERCISE 13

‖: C | Am | F | G :‖

Now for a song; first, let's look at one you already know in G: "Will the Circle Be Unbroken."

WILL THE CIRCLE BE UNBROKEN — KEY OF C

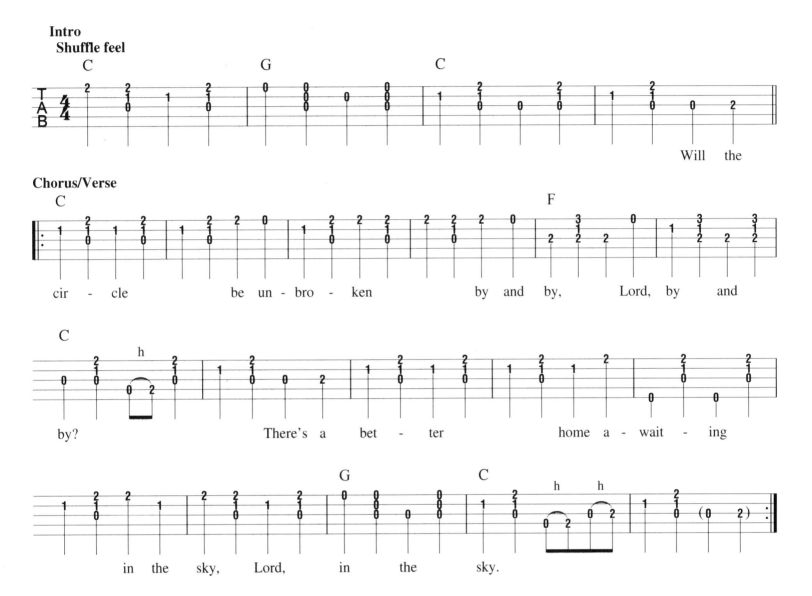

Playing Notes:

- It's still only three chords, but this time it's C, F, and G instead of G, C, and D7.

- If playing in C is new to you, strum the song and sing or hum it until the chords feel comfortable before you add in any melody notes.

- All the strums are down-strums.

- Leave the last two notes off to end the song.

"The Fox" is a traditional song dating back hundreds of years, but it has lasting power, having been recorded by such greats as Pete Seeger, Harry Belafonte, the Smothers Brothers, and more recently, Nickel Creek.

THE FOX

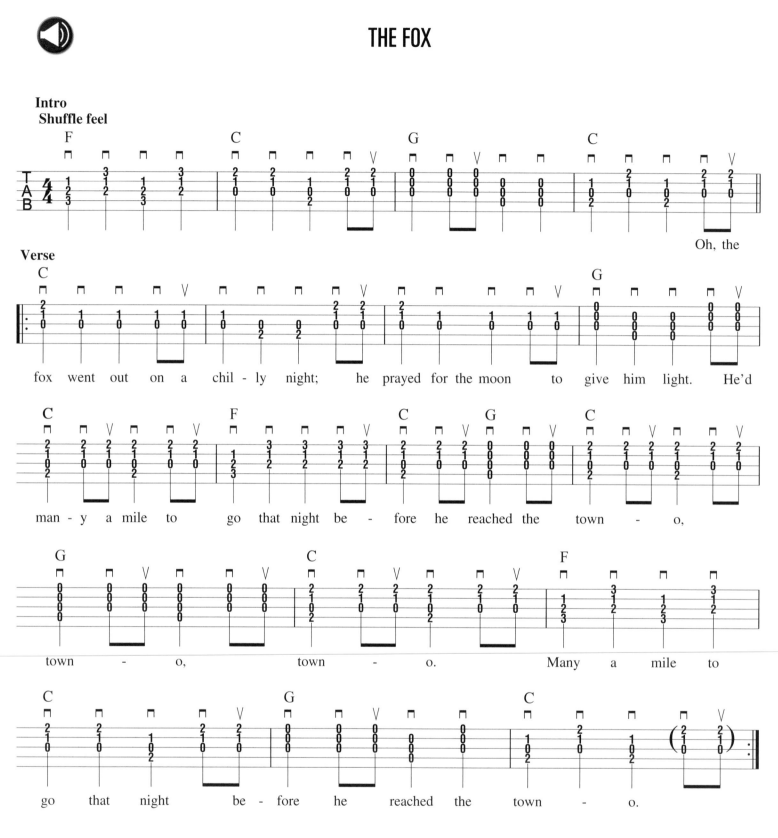

Additional Lyrics:

He ran till he came to the farmer's pen.
The ducks and the geese were kept therein.
He said a couple of you are gonna grease my chin
Before I leave this town-o, town-o, town-o.
A couple of you are gonna grease my chin
Before I leave this town-o.

Playing Notes:

- It's only three chords: C, F, and G.

- You can play the chords with any strumming or note-strum, etc., patterns, and you can try the arrangement supplied here. This arrangement is all strumming, but with a couple of differences: it breaks out of the patterns and it breaks up the strums to groups of two strings. This works great for this song because all the melody notes are in the chords.

- Don't worry too much about hitting the exact notes in the tab, but try to include the strings with the melody notes. And go ahead and strum the 5th string on the full down-strums if you want.

- While it can be sung and played slowly and sweetly, my favorite versions are fast and bouncy. Try it at different tempos to see what you like. If you play it quickly, give it a good bounce.

- Leave the last two strums off to end the song.

CHAPTER 11:
CHORDS AND SONGS IN THE KEY OF D

Another key that you'll want to familiarize yourself with is the key of D. Here's an expanded chart to show how to change chords in songs between G, C, and D:

Numbers	I	ii	iii	IV	V	vi
Key of G	G	Am	Bm	C	D or D7	Em
Key of C	C	Dm	Em	F	G or G7	Am
Key of D	D	Em	F#m	G	A or A7	Bm

CHANGING THE 5TH STRING

When playing in D, it's usually a good idea to raise the 5th string from G to A. If you have hooks installed on your banjo, hook it so it rests on the fret that's two higher than the open 5th string. If you don't have hooks installed, you can just tune it up. But be careful when you do, and keep your face away from the strings; it's possible that the string might break, and the end could poke whatever's near! And be sure to change it back to G before you play a song in G or C!

NEW CHORDS FOR THE KEY OF D

You already know most of the chords in D. Here are the ones that may be new to you:

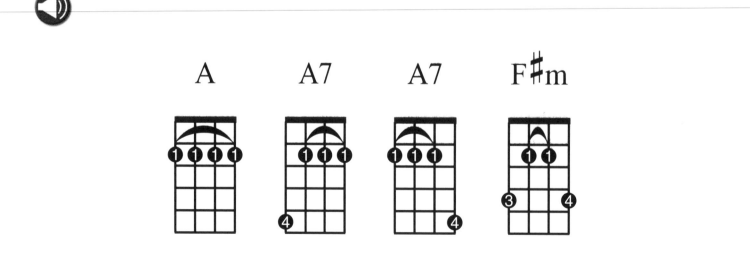

Hints:

- For the A and A7, hold down all four long strings with your index finger by laying the side of it across the 2nd fret. This is called a *barre* and is indicated in the chord grids with a curved line.

- Note that this A chord is the same shape as the G chord; you just use your index finger to raise all four strings by two frets. The A7 chords are the same shape as the G7 chords as well.

- For F♯ minor, hold down either strings 2 and 3, or 1 through 4 with your index finger. Note that the F♯ minor is really the same shape as the Em, with all the strings raised by two frets.

CHORD EXERCISES

The following exercises will help you get comfortable playing these new chords. Try to use both versions of the A7 chord.

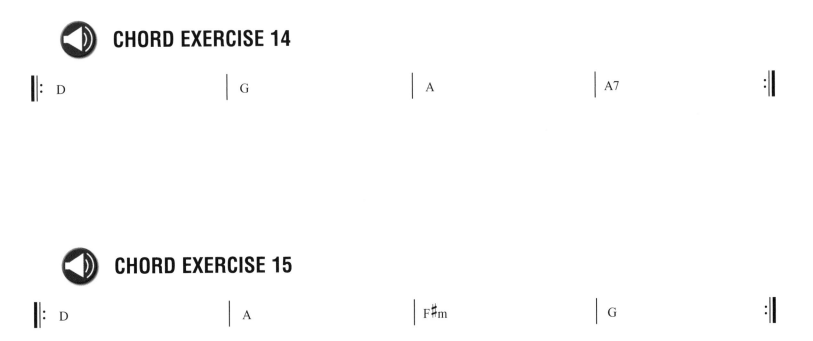

CHORD EXERCISE 14

‖: D | G | A | A7 :‖

CHORD EXERCISE 15

‖: D | A | F♯m | G :‖

Here's "The Fox" again, this time in D.

THE FOX – KEY OF D

Playing Notes:

- Strumming a melody works in D as well as C (and G).

- Try using your pinky to play the 5th fret of the 1st string on the G chords. If your pinky won't cooperate, use your ring finger.

A traditional song from Ireland or Scotland, depending on who you ask, "Handsome Molly" is known by many names, including "Irish Girl," "Lovely Molly," "Dark-Eyed Molly," and "Going to Mass Last Sunday."

This strum pattern works well for this song:

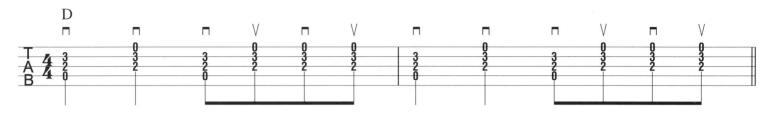

Here's a mostly note-strum arrangement with much of the melody.

HANDSOME MOLLY

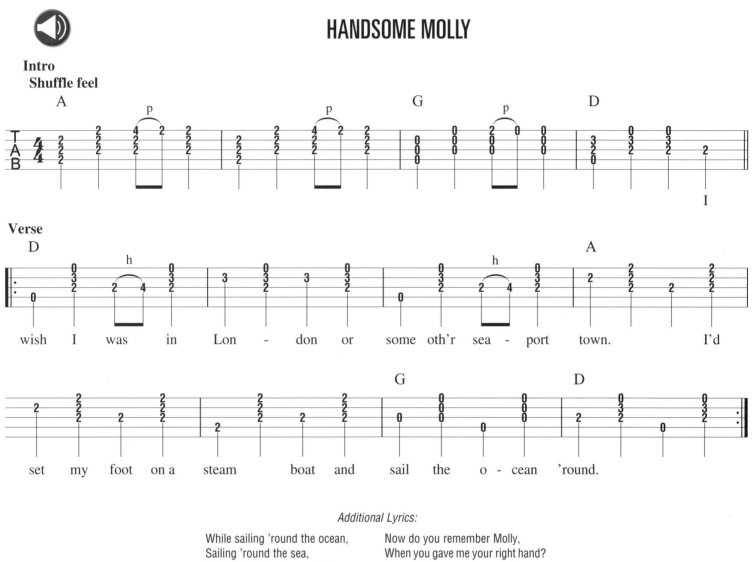

wish I was in Lon - don or some oth'r sea - port town. I'd

set my foot on a steam boat and sail the o - cean 'round.

Additional Lyrics:

While sailing 'round the ocean,
Sailing 'round the sea,
I'd think of Handsome Molly
Wherever she may be.

I saw her at church last Sunday;
Molly she passed me by.
I knew her mind was changing
By the roving of her eye.

Now do you remember Molly,
When you gave me your right hand?
You said if you ever married
I would be your man.

Now you've broke your promise.
Go marry whom you please.
My poor heart is broken
While you are at your ease.

Playing Notes:

- This song works well with a steady strum using a pattern like the suggested one.

- You can leave off the last strum to end the song if you like, or play it.

CHAPTER 12:
USING A CAPO TO PLAY IN OTHER KEYS

Now you can play a few songs in three different keys: G, C, and D. What about the other keys? What if you want to play with a singer who insists that she sing a song in the key of A? Or B flat?

With banjo—and a capo—it's no problem! One of the great things about fretted string instruments is that if you can play a song in one key—G, for instance—you can use a capo to change it to other keys. As an example, we'll change from G to A.

Here's a chord chart showing the chords in G and A:

Numbers	I	ii	iii	IV	V	vi
Key of G	G	Am	Bm	C	D or D7	Em
Key of A	A	Bm	C#m	D	E or E7	F#m

So, the I, IV, and V chords in A are: A, D, and E or E7. Here's a diagram of the I, IV, and V chords in both G and A, this time using a capo for A.

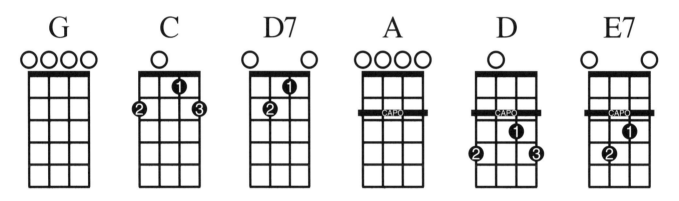

See how the three main chords in G become the three main chords in A, just by putting on the capo and playing the same chord shapes? The A is the same shape (no fingers on frets) as the G. The capo raises all four strings to form an A chord. The D chord is shaped like a C, but the capo raises the whole chord to a D. And the E7 is shaped just like a D7, but the capo raises the whole chord to an E7.

So, if you put a capo on the 2nd fret and play anything you learned in G—strum, note-strum, note-strum-thumb, fingerpicking, or any other style or technique—you transpose what you play to the key of A.

And if you can play something in D, with a capo on the 2nd fret it will sound in E, which is a good key for many male singers.

SAME FINGERING, DIFFERENT CHORDS

Using a capo can be confusing at first. Look at the D chord in the diagram above. It looks and feels like a C chord, but because it has been raised two frets, it's now a D. And if the capo is on another fret, it'll be a different chord. Just be patient. The more you use a capo, the sooner it'll become less confusing.

INSTALLING A CAPO

There are many kinds of capos, and they all attach a little differently. The main thing is to make sure they are close to the fret—but not overlapping it—and that they're tight enough that the strings ring cleanly but not so tight that they pull the strings sharp. Like most things, this will take a little practice.

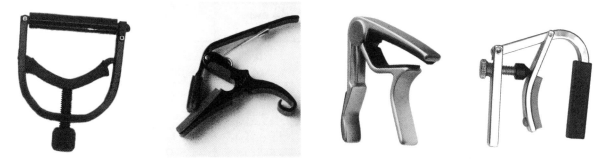

Here are just a few of your capo options, including some guitar capos, which will work if that's all that's handy.

IMPORTANT! DON'T FORGET THE 5TH STRING!

A very important thing to remember about using a capo with a five-string banjo is that you may also need to change the 5th string. That 5th string is a ringing drone, so it has to be a note that sounds good with all (or at least most) of the chords in the key you're playing.

The general rule is this: *however many frets you raise the four long strings with a capo, you must also raise the 5th string.*

You can raise the 5th string by tuning it up. But be careful: you can't tune it up very far (not more than two frets or so) without breaking it. So if you find that you want to play in keys where you have to raise it more than two frets, take your banjo to a music store or luthier and have *hooks* installed.

When capoing something that you play in the key of D, where you raise the 5th string by two frets, you have to use that as your starting point. So if you are in D and you've already hooked the 5th string up two frets, then if you put the capo on the 2nd fret, you have to raise the 5th string two more frets.

There are other options for changing the 5th string beyond the general rule. For the most part, you want the drone to be tuned to a note that is either the root (1) or the 5th (or sometimes the 3rd) of the key you're playing in. For example, in the key of A, the 5th string should be tuned to A (root) or E (5th). A is closer to the starting point of G, so that's the more logical choice.

Sometimes, it's easier to tune the 5th string down instead of up. For the key of F, the 5th string should be F or C. Depending on the sound you want, you may hook it five frets up to make a C (don't try tuning it that far!), or you may lower the string from G to F.

KEY CHANGE CHART

Here's a chart that will help you use a capo to change songs in the keys of G, C, and D into other keys. The more common keys are shown in bold letters. Most players rarely capo above the 4th fret, but you can go to the 7th fret or beyond if you need or want to.

The far left column gives the keys as played with no capo. The other columns show what each of those three keys changes to at frets 1 through 7. Below each key are one or two suggested ways to change the 5th string. A "+0" means you don't change it: leave it at a G.

	Capo on Fret						
No Capo	**1**	**2**	**3**	**4**	**5**	**6**	**7**
G +0	G# or A♭ +1	**A** +2	A# or **B**♭ +3	**B** +4	**C** +0 or +5	C# or D♭ +1 or +6	**D** +2 or +7
C +0	C# or D♭ +1	**D** +2	D# or E♭ +3	**E** +4	**F** -2 or +5	F# or G♭ -1 or +6	**G** +0 or +7
D +2	D# or E♭ +3	**E** +4	**F** +5 or -2	F# or G♭ +6 or -1	**G** +7 or +0	G# or A♭ +1	**A** +2

Notice that, for a number of keys, there is more than one place to play. For instance, you can play in the key of C without a capo, and you can play in the key of C with a capo on the 5th fret using the chord shapes for the key of G. When you play in these two positions, the chords are the same chords, but they sound a little different. One set has higher notes, and the notes of the chords are in a different order. (Playing chords with the notes in different order is called playing different *inversions*.) If you're playing with another banjo player or guitar player, you can use this to your advantage: one person plays the chords without a capo; the other plays the same chords with a capo. Together, they make a big, full sound—Peter, Paul, and Mary made good use of this technique with two guitars.

YOUR ASSIGNMENT

Try playing any of the songs you've learned so far from this book—or any other songs you know and like—in different keys using a capo. In particular, try playing "Cripple Creek" in A (chords from the key of G, capoed up two frets). If you play with a fiddler, they'll always want to play "Cripple Creek" in A.

CHAPTER 13: FINGERPICKING PATTERNS

In folk style banjo, there are a number of different ways to fingerpick. We can't cover them all here, but we can make a good start. In this book, we'll explore three-finger picking: we'll use the thumb (t), the index (i), and the middle (m) fingers to pluck the strings. There are styles that use two fingers (thumb and index) as well as four fingers (thumb, index, middle, and ring), but these days three-finger picking is the most common.

When fingerpicking, your thumb plucks strings in a downward motion, and your fingers pluck upward. For this chapter, you may use a thumbpick and bare fingers, or a thumbpick and fingerpicks if you desire.

One approach to fingerpicking is to use picking patterns to play chords just as you do with strumming patterns. Here are a few useful patterns. The first six have a four count, and the last four have a three count. Practice them until you can play them smoothly, and then try them with the chord exercises in the previous chapters. In all of these patterns, use your middle finger to play the 1st string and your index finger to play the 2nd string. Your thumb plays all the notes on the 3rd, 4th, and 5th strings.

🔊 PICKING PATTERN 1

🔊 PICKING PATTERN 2

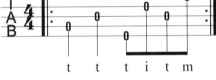

🔊 PICKING PATTERN 3

PICKING PATTERN 4

PICKING PATTERN 5

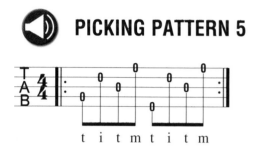

PICKING PATTERN 6

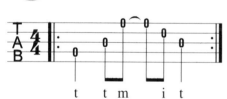

PICKING PATTERN 7

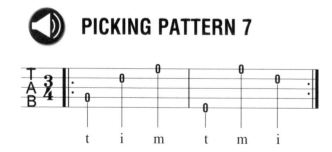

PICKING PATTERN 8

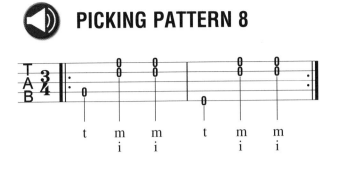

PICKING PATTERN 9

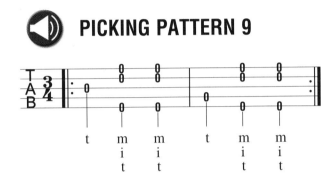

PICKING PATTERN 10

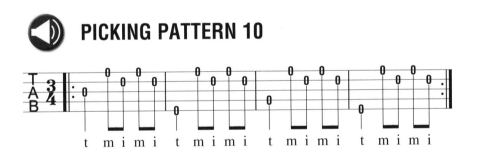

These are just a few of the many possible patterns you can play. Start with these, and then experiment and find some more patterns that you like.

PATTERNS ON A SONG

You can play a single pattern for a whole song, and it'll sound just fine. The goal is to support the singer, so keeping it clean and simple is often a good way to go. But there are times when you may want to fancy it up a little, mixing and matching patterns to add interest and have some fun. One approach is to use a different pattern for each chord. For example, if you played "Will the Circle Be Unbroken" in G, you could use Pattern 2 for all the G chords, Pattern 3 for the C chords, and Pattern 5 for the D7 chords. Try it.

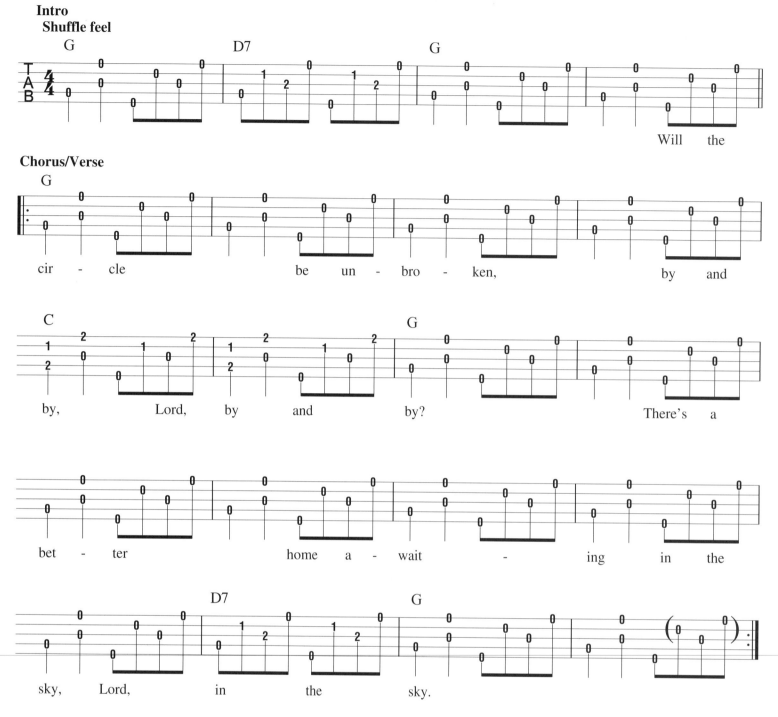

Playing Notes:

- Leave off the last three notes to end the song.

- Try substituting other patterns on the three chords.

- Try these and other patterns on the other songs in this book or any other songs you know and like. Take some time to experiment and play around before moving on.

CHAPTER 14: CONNECTING CHORDS WITH RUNS

Another useful technique is to pick patterns on the chords and connect the chords with runs. *Runs* are short musical phrases—usually just a few notes—that lead from one chord to the next. (They are called bass runs when played on guitar because they're usually played on the lower-pitched strings.)

When fingerpicking, runs can (but don't have to) be played with the thumb, as in the examples that follow.

THE IV–I–V–I PROGRESSION

Your introduction to runs will be with the versatile IV–I–V–I progression. Many songs use this progression, including "Midnight Special," "This Land Is Your Land," and dozens more. It uses the usual three chords—I, IV, and V—as shown in the chart below for the keys of G, C, and D.

Numbers	IV	I	V	I
Key of G	C	G	D or D7	G
Key of C	F	C	G or G7	C
Key of D	G	D	A or A7	D

The first run example is in G. All the run notes (except one) are played with the thumb. The index and middle fingers work together to fill in chord notes between the run notes.

 RUNS EXAMPLE 1

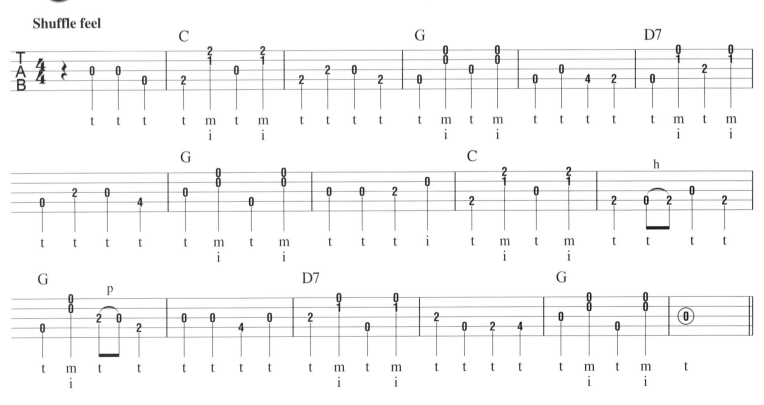

Playing Notes:

- There are lots of places where you use your index and middle fingers together.

- There's just one hammer-on and one pull-off here, but there's room to add more if you want.

This next example uses picking patterns to fill in chord notes between the runs.

RUNS EXAMPLE 2

Shuffle feel

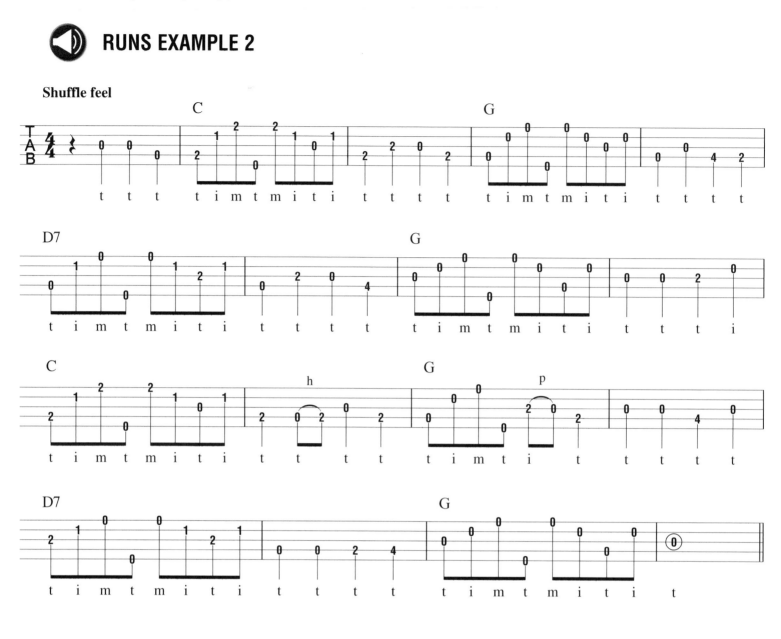

Playing Notes:

- Almost all the runs are played with the thumb, except for one pull-off that is plucked with the index finger.

Here's a run example in the key of C using the same progression.

RUNS EXAMPLE 3

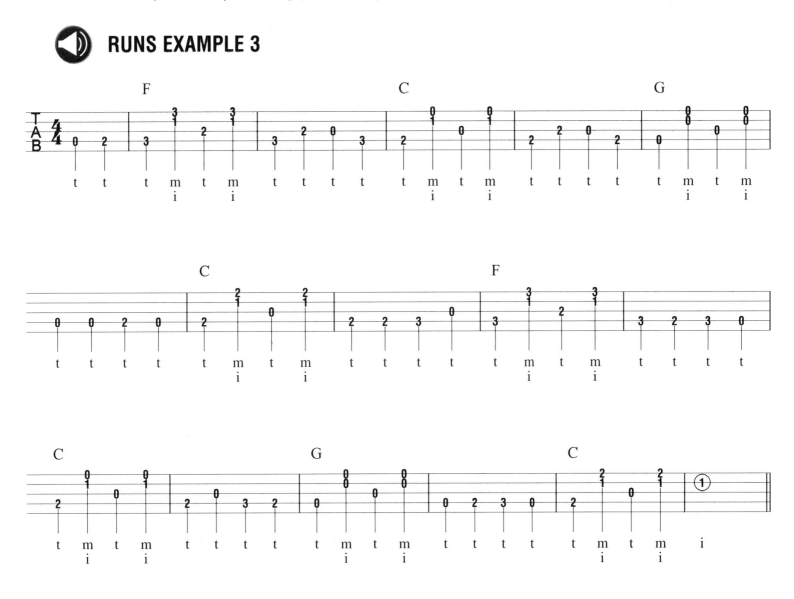

Playing Notes:

- If playing in C is still new to you, first play this one a few times without the runs: pick or strum the chords until they feel comfortable.

- When playing this one with runs, as you change chords—especially to F and C—finger the whole chord to start with. Then move or lift fingers as needed to play the runs.

And here it is in the key of D. Tune or hook your 5th string up two frets while playing in D.

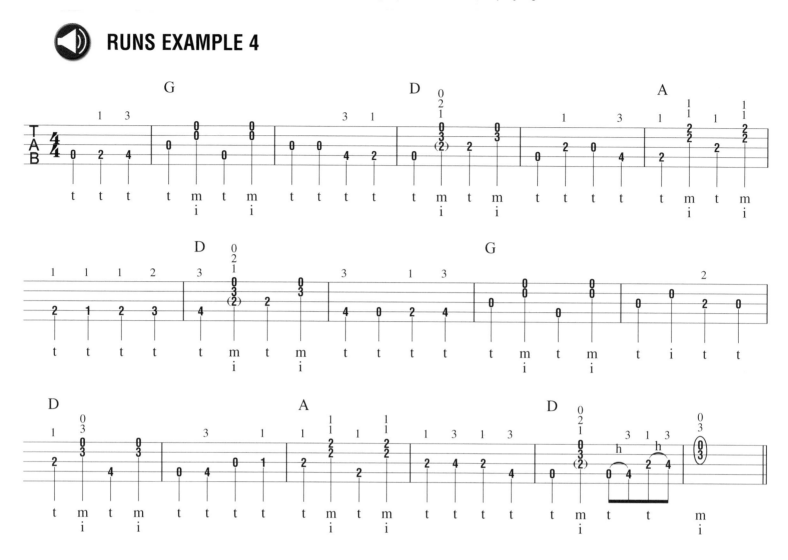

RUNS EXAMPLE 4

Playing Notes:

- If playing in D is new to you, first play this one a few times without the runs: pick or strum the chords until they feel comfortable.

- This one may have you doing new shapes and movements with your fingers, so pay attention to the fingering.

- When playing this one with runs, as you change chords—especially to D and A—finger the whole chord to start with and continue to hold that chord until you need to move a finger to play a run or change chords.

- When playing the A chords, hold down (barre) all four strings with your index finger (1).

- Notice the note in parentheses on the 2nd fret of the 3rd string in three of the D measures. You don't play that note, but you put your finger there so it's in position to play the note when it's needed.

- Two of the runs in this one are *chromatic*, meaning they have notes outside the major scale.

- Pay attention to the fingering on the runs. It gets a little tricky at times.

These are just a few examples of runs. Listen for runs when you hear other banjo players play and try to incorporate them into songs when you practice.

CHAPTER 15:
PICKING WITH ADDED MELODY

During an instrumental break, or even while accompanying a singer, you may want to add a little melody to your picking. Previously, you picked a melody and filled in between the lines or long notes with chord strums. You can also pick a melody and fill in between the lines and longer notes by picking patterns or parts of patterns over the chords.

Here's a nice, pretty, slow picking version of "Down in the Valley." The melody is mostly played with the thumb.

DOWN IN THE VALLEY – MELODY AND PICKING

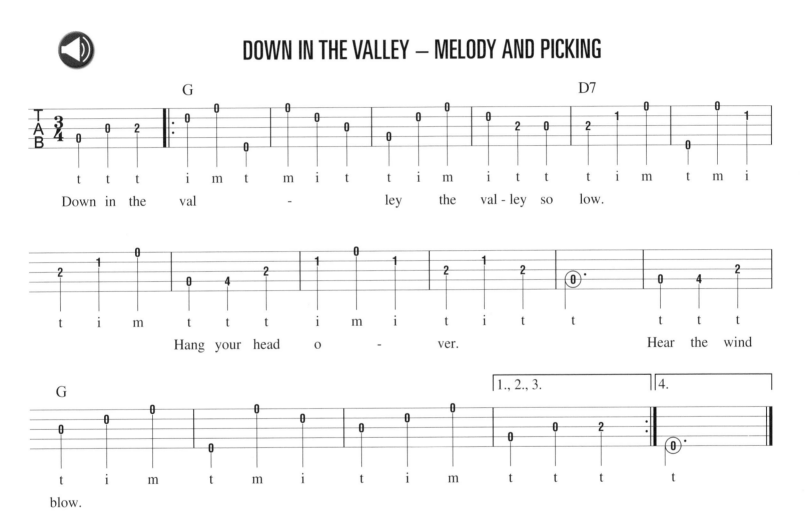

Playing Notes:

- The fills are played by the index (i) and middle (m) fingers on the 1st and 2nd strings. The thumb (t) plays the other strings.

Here's another approach to playing melody: use the index and middle fingers together through most of the song to get a nice, full sound. No lyrics are provided; you should be able to hear the melody clearly when you play it. Pay attention to the plucking hand fingering.

OH! SUSANNA — INDEX AND MIDDLE TOGETHER

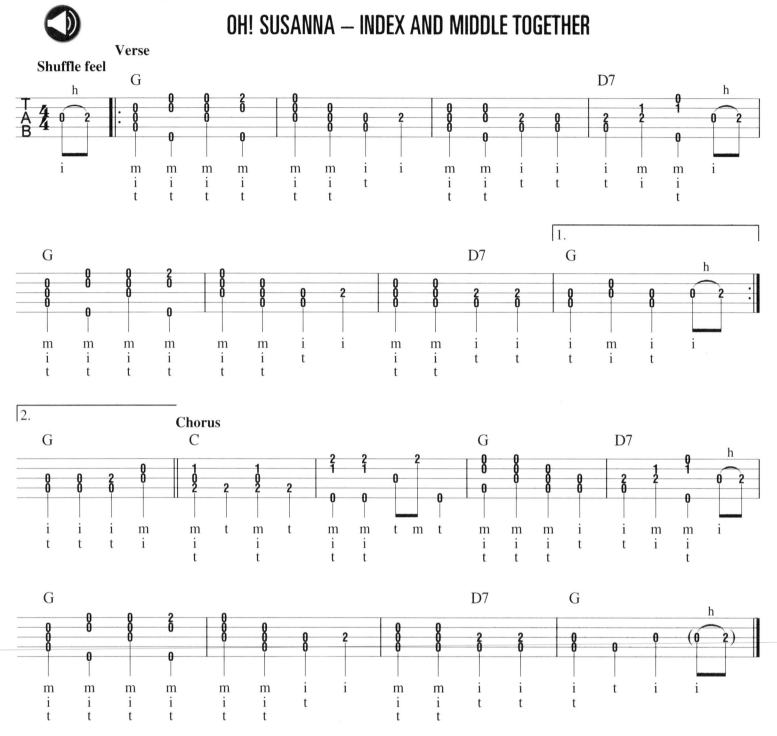

Playing Notes:

- There's one little fill in the chorus where the i and m fingers don't play together. You can add other fills like this if you want.

- Leave off the last two notes to end the song.

"Home Sweet Home" has been around for over 150 years. It was popular with soldiers from both the North and South during the Civil War and has found its way into the soundtracks of many movies and cartoons. Today, it's part of the standard bluegrass repertoire, having been played by Earl Scruggs, Béla Fleck, and many others. It has lyrics, but these days you mostly hear it as an instrumental.

In this arrangement, the melody is played, and parts of picking patterns are used to fill in the spaces between the melody notes.

HOME, SWEET HOME

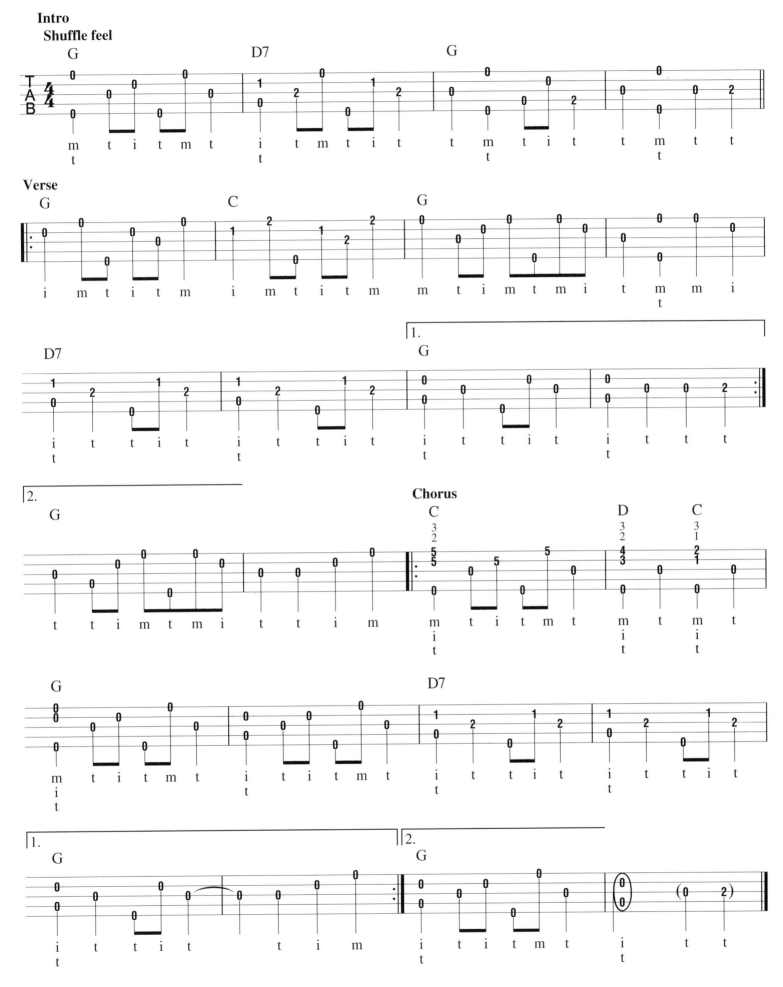

Playing Notes:

- Note the fretting-hand fingering in the first measure of the chorus. Keep your ring and middle fingers on the 5th fret of the 1st and 2nd strings for the whole first measure. In the beginning of the next measure, keep the fingers on the same strings and slide the ring finger down to the 4th fret and the middle finger down to the 3rd fret. To finish the measure, slide the ring finger down to the 2nd fret and use your index finger on the 1st fret of the 2nd string—just as you would when holding a C chord.

- Try to bring out the melody notes; play them louder than the fill notes.

- Try to come up with other fills.

- Leave off the last two notes to end the song.

CHAPTER 16: WHERE ARE YOU NOW AND WHERE ARE YOU GOING?

You're at the end of the book. It's time to evaluate your progress.

The most important thing to remember is that *any progress is good*. Different people absorb this material at different speeds, depending on their previous music experience, their available time to practice, and their desire to learn. Playing music should be fun. It takes some work and dedication to make progress, but don't forget to have fun; sing, play, and play with others.

If you can play all the chords, all the strums (and variations), all the picking patterns, and most of the arrangements in this book smoothly, then congratulations! You're ready to learn more songs and have more fun with the banjo. You may also want to explore other banjo techniques, such as Scruggs-style picking and clawhammer.

If you can play most of the chords, a few strums and picking patterns, and a song or two, then… congratulations! You've made progress. There's still a lot in this book that can be useful to you, so go back and find the places that gave you trouble and spend a little time there. But you should also take what you already know and apply it to other songs. Find songs that you like—folk or not—and learn to play them.

However much you learned from this book, you may also want to find a local teacher who can help you out with the tricky parts and give you feedback and encouragement.

BEYOND THIS BOOK

Beyond the songs in this book, you can apply all these techniques to thousands of others—folk songs and others as well. If you're playing for a sing-along, then you'll want to play songs that people will know. If your friends are traditional folkies, you'll play folk songs. But you may also want to play modern songs that your friends will know the words to.

IMPROVING YOUR MUSICIANSHIP

The best (and possibly most fun) way to improve your musicianship is to play with other people. Find singers to play with or find other musicians to jam with. Let them know what songs you already know, but also ask what they like to sing or play and learn those songs.

Another great way to improve your musicianship is to figure out how to play simple melodies from memory. Hum the tune and then find the notes on the banjo. Start with the simplest songs—like nursery rhymes—then slowly work your way up to more complicated songs.

Many people have a hard time figuring out the chords to songs. Of course, you can find the chords to millions of songs in books and sheet music, but it's useful to be able to figure them out when you need them. Start with two-chord songs like "Skip to My Lou," "Buffalo Gals," "Clementine," "Jambalaya," "Mary Had a Little Lamb," and "Tom Dooley."

HOW TO LEARN NEW SONGS

Here's a proven way to learn new songs effectively:

1. Listen to the song as many times as it takes to be able to hum or sing it to yourself.

2. Feel the rhythm. Count it and then deaden the strings and strum along with it.

3. Listen to hear when the chords change.

4. Get the chords. If you can figure them out yourself, that's great. If not, ask a friend or find them in a songbook. In the folk world, you'll only need the three or four (sometimes only two) most basic chords for any key. Some rock and pop tunes are more complex.

5. Play just the chords as you sing or hum the song. Try different playing styles and various picking and strumming patterns.

6. Pick out the melody notes. Take your time and be patient.

7. Try to combine the chords and melody.

8. Play it over and over and over.

ACKNOWLEDGMENTS

This book is dedicated to the great folk musicians of the world, famous and obscure, who keep this music alive, with a special shout out to Pete Seeger for being a musical and banjo inspiration to so many of us players.

I'd like to thank all the musicians I have the honor to play with, including those in the bands the Buffalo Gals West, Rush Creek, Sgt. Funky, and the Corn Mountain Steamers, as well as the Mountain Fiddlers Jam and the Nevada County Banjo Summit.

I also thank the people at Hal Leonard, including Jeff Schroedl and Kurt Plahna, for their support and for helping people all over the world learn to play music.

Above all, I thank my wonderful wife, Linda, for her support and for putting up with my banjo playing (and my looks) every day for the last ten years and the next fifty.

ABOUT THE AUTHOR

Michael Bremer actually remembers the 1960s and grew up listening to—and loving—the folk music of that era, both new and traditional. Today, he makes his living through words, music, and teaching. As a writer, editor, and publisher, he has worked on projects ranging from computer games to medical equipment to online math courses to music instruction.

As a musician, he has played guitar since 1968. In 2002, he moved to the Sierra Nevada foothills in Northern California and decided it was time to learn banjo. It took over his musical world. Today, he plays banjo (and some guitar) in a number of bands that play everything from old time to swing to rock 'n' roll (yes, he plays electric banjo in a rock band—but don't tell the California Bluegrass Association). He also writes songs and believes it's time for banjo to re-enter the world of singer-songwriters. Through it all, Michael is a compulsive teacher, holding workshops and seminars for writers as well as banjo players, and has taught classes at the California Bluegrass Association Music Camp.

Combining his instructional writing, his love of music (especially banjo), and teaching, he began writing and producing a series of instructional books and videos, which is what brought him to the attention of Hal Leonard and led to this book.

GREAT BANJO PUBLICATIONS

FROM HAL LEONARD CORPORATION

Hal Leonard Banjo Method – Second Edition
by Mac Robertson, Robbie Clement, Will Schmid
This innovative method teaches 5-string banjo blue-grass style using a carefully paced approach that keeps beginners playing great songs *while learning*. Book 1 covers easy chord strums, tablature, right-hand rolls, hammer-ons, slides and pull-offs, and more. Book 2 includes solos and licks, fiddle tunes, back-up, capo use, and more.
00699500 Book 1 (Book Only).................................. $7.99
00695101 Book 1 (Book/CD Pack) $16.99
00699502 Book 2 (Book Only................................. $7.99

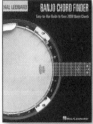

Banjo Chord Finder
This extensive reference guide covers over 2,800 banjo chords, including four of the most commonly used tunings. Thirty different chord qualities are covered for each key, and each chord quality is presented in two different voicings. Also includes a lesson on chord construction and a fingerboard chart of the banjo neck!

00695741 9 x 12... $6.99
00695742 6 x 9... $5.95

Banjo Scale Finder
by Chad Johnson
Learn to play scales on the banjo with this compre-hensive yet easy-to-use book. It contains more than 1,300 scale diagrams for the most often-used scales and modes, including multiple patterns for each scale. Also includes a lesson on scale construction and a fingerboard chart of the banjo neck.

00695780 9 x 12... $6.95
00695783 6 x 9... $5.95

The Beatles for Banjo
18 of the Fab Four's finest for five string banjo! Includes: Across the Universe • Blackbird • A Hard Day's Night • Here Comes the Sun • Hey Jude • Let It Be • She Loves You • Strawberry Fields Forever • Ticket to Ride • Yesterday • and more.

00700813 ....$14.99

Christmas Favorites for Banjo
27 holiday classics arranged for banjo, including: Blue Christmas • Feliz Navidad • Frosty the Snow Man • Grandma's Killer Fruitcake • A Holly Jolly Christmas • I Saw Mommy Kissing Santa Claus • It's Beginning to Look like Christmas • Jingle-Bell Rock • Nuttin' for Christmas • Rudolph the Red-Nosed Reindeer • Silver Bells • and more.

00699109... $10.95

Fretboard Roadmaps
by Fred Sokolow
This handy book/CD pack will get you playing all over the banjo fretboard in any key! You'll learn to: increase your chord, scale and lick vocabu-lary • play chord-based licks, moveable major and blues scales, melodic scales and first-position major scales • and much more! The CD includes 51 dem-onstrations of the exercises.
00695358 Book/CD Pack $14.95

O Brother, Where Art Thou?
Banjo tab arrangements of 12 bluegrass/folk songs from this Grammy-winning album. Includes: The Big Rock Candy Mountain • Down to the River to Pray • I Am a Man of Constant Sorrow • I Am Weary (Let Me Rest) • I'll Fly Away • In the Jailhouse Now • Keep on the Sunny Side • You Are My Sunshine • and more, plus lyrics and a banjo notation legend.

00699528 Banjo Tablature.. $12.95

Earl Scruggs and the 5-String Banjo
Earl Scruggs' legendary method has helped thou-sands of banjo players get their start. It features everything you need to know to start playing, even how to build your own banjo! Topics covered include: Scruggs tuners • how to read music • chords • how to read tablature • anatomy of Scruggs-style picking • exercises in picking • 44 songs • biographi-cal notes • and more! The CD features Earl Scruggs playing and explaining over 60 examples!
00695764 Book Only.. $19.95
00695765 Book/CD Pack $34.99

The Tony Trischka Collection
59 authentic transciptions by Tony Trischka, one of the world's best banjo pickers and instruc-tors. Includes: Blown Down Wall • China Grove • Crossville Breakdown • Heartlands • Hill Country • Kentucky Bullfight • A Robot Plane Flies over Arkansas • and more. Features an introduction by Béla Fleck, plus Tony's comments on each song. Transcriptions are in tab only.
00699063 Banjo Tablature... $19.95

The Ultimate Banjo Songbook
A great collection of banjo classics: Alabama Jubilee • Bye Bye Love • Duelin' Banjos • The Entertainer • Foggy Mountain Breakdown • Great Balls of Fire • Lady of Spain • Orange Blossom Special • (Ghost) Riders in the Sky • Rocky Top • San Antonio Rose • Tennessee Waltz • UFO-TOFU • You Are My Sunshine • and more.

00699565 Book/2-CD Pack $24.95

Prices, contents, and availability subject to change without notice.

Visit Hal Leonard online at **www.halleonard.com**

0514